# Agile ENTERPRISE SOLUTION ARCHITECTURE

## — An IT Service-Based Modeling Approach

SEAN GU

The author and publisher have taken care in the preparation of this book, but make no expressed or implied warranty of any kind and assume no responsibility for errors or omissions. No liability is assumed for incidental or consequential damages in connection with or arising out of the use of the information or programs contained herein.

Publisher: Vernal Press
Proofreader: Jake Magnum, et al.

To obtain permission to use material from this work or require related assistance, please send an email request to: vernalpress@outlook.com.

ISBN: 978-0-578-83097-1
1st Printing: April 2021

# DEDICATION

*To my mom, Autumn Moon,*

*for always loving and inspiring me.*


*To my fellow geeks,*

*for better applying practical IT architecture.*

# CONTENTS

INTRODUCTION ............................................................................................................ 1

CHAPTER 1: A-ESA FRAMEWORK ............................................................................ 4

  1.1 THE NATURE OF IT SERVICES ................................................................................. 5

  1.2 MODEL COVERAGE AND INTENT ........................................................................... 7

  1.3 MODEL FRAMEWORK ............................................................................................ 9

    *1.3.1 Model Area* .................................................................................................. 11

    *1.3.2 Model View* ................................................................................................. 12

    *1.3.3 Model Element* ........................................................................................... 16

    *1.3.4 Model Property* ........................................................................................... 18

  1.4 MODELING FOR CHANGE ..................................................................................... 18

CHAPTER 2: A-ESA AREAS AND VIEWS ................................................................ 21

  2.1 ENTERPRISE AREA ............................................................................................... 21

    *2.1.1 Capability View* .......................................................................................... 22

    *2.1.2 Organization View* ..................................................................................... 23

  2.2 CASE SCENARIO AREA ......................................................................................... 24

    *2.2.1 Use Case Model View* ................................................................................. 25

    *2.2.2 Process View* .............................................................................................. 26

    *2.2.3 Page Flow View* .......................................................................................... 27

  2.3 ARCHITECTURE OVERVIEW AREA ......................................................................... 28

    *2.3.1 Outline View* ............................................................................................... 29

    *2.3.2 Pattern View* ............................................................................................... 32

    *2.3.3 Metrics View* ............................................................................................... 33

    *2.3.4 DevOps View* .............................................................................................. 34

    *2.3.5 Relationship Validation View* ..................................................................... 34

  2.4 FUNCTIONAL SERVICE AREA ............................................................................... 36

    *2.4.1 Service Relationship View* ........................................................................... 38

    *2.4.2 Service Interaction View* ............................................................................. 38

    *2.4.3 Service Component Realization View* .......................................................... 39

  2.5 INFRASTRUCTURAL AREA .................................................................................... 40

    *2.5.1 Package Mapping View* ............................................................................... 41

    *2.5.2 Deployment View* ....................................................................................... 42

CHAPTER 3: A-ESA ELEMENTS .............................................................................. 44

3.1 Enterprise Elements.................................................................................48
    3.1.1 Capability Element.........................................................................48
3.2 Case Scenario Elements.........................................................................49
    3.2.1 Role Element...............................................................................49
    3.2.2 Use Case Element.........................................................................49
    3.2.3 Task Element..............................................................................50
3.3 Metrics Elements.................................................................................51
    3.3.1 Architecture Principle Element........................................................51
    3.3.2 Requirement Element.....................................................................53
    3.3.3 Key Choice Element......................................................................55
    3.3.4 Risk Element.............................................................................58
    3.3.5 Governance Element......................................................................58
3.4 Functional Elements.............................................................................59
    3.4.1 GUI Service Element......................................................................61
    3.4.2 Application Logic Service Element......................................................61
    3.4.3 Data Service Element....................................................................62
    3.4.4 Technical Service Element..............................................................64
    3.4.5 Service Interface Element..............................................................64
    3.4.6 Service Component Element..............................................................66
3.5 Infrastructural Elements.......................................................................67
    3.5.1 Package Element..........................................................................67
    3.5.2 Middleware Element......................................................................68
    3.5.3 System Element...........................................................................70
    3.5.4 Node Element.............................................................................71
    3.5.5 Network Element.........................................................................71
    3.5.6 Location Element.........................................................................72
3.6 Connection Elements.............................................................................72
    3.6.1 Association Relationship Element.......................................................73
    3.6.2 Flow Relationship Element..............................................................73
    3.6.3 Composition Relationship Element......................................................74
    3.6.4 Realization Relationship Element.......................................................74
3.7 General Elements.................................................................................74
    3.7.1 Generic Service Element................................................................74
    3.7.2 Note Element.............................................................................76
    3.7.3 View Frame Element......................................................................76
    3.7.4 Group Element............................................................................77
    3.7.5 Domain Element...........................................................................77
3.8 Assistive Representation Elements.............................................................79
    3.8.1 Cloud Service Element...................................................................80

*3.8.2 Product Element* ........................................................................... *81*

*3.8.3 Application Element* ..................................................................... *82*

*3.8.4 Mobile Device Element* ................................................................ *82*

*3.8.5 DB Store Element* ........................................................................ *83*

*3.8.6 Composite/Process Service Element* ........................................ *83*

*3.8.7 Virtual Service Element* .............................................................. *83*

*3.8.8 Extension Element* ....................................................................... *84*

CHAPTER 4: AN A-ESA CASE STUDY ................................................... 86

4.1 CASE BACKGROUND.......................................................................... 86

4.2 SOLUTION ARCHITECTURE VIEWS ................................................... 88

*4.2.1 Enterprise Capability Area* ......................................................... *89*

*4.2.2 Case Scenario Area* ..................................................................... *92*

*4.2.3 Architecture Overview Area* ....................................................... *96*

*4.2.4 Functional Area*............................................................................ *112*

*4.2.5 Infrastructural Area* ..................................................................... *120*

CHAPTER 5: IT ARCHITECTURE ASSESSMENT .................................. 130

5.1 ASSESSMENT INTENT AND SCOPE .................................................. 130

*5.1.1 Assessment Situation*.................................................................. *130*

*5.1.2 Assessment Scope*........................................................................ *133*

*5.1.3 Assessment Criteria* ..................................................................... *133*

5.2 AN ASSESSMENT WALKTHROUGH ................................................... 135

*5.2.1 Architectural Checklist* ............................................................... *135*

*5.2.2 Model Enhancement*.................................................................... *139*

*5.2.3 Further Enhancement Work* ....................................................... *148*

EPILOGUE................................................................................................ 149

APPENDIX I: TEXT CONVENTIONS ....................................................... 151

APPENDIX II: VIEW ABBREVIATION ..................................................... 152

APPENDIX III: ELEMENT LIST ............................................................... 153

APPENDIX IV: ELEMENT RELATIONSHIP ............................................. 156

APPENDIX V: ARCHIMATE MAPPING ................................................... 157

APPENDIX VI: SOA COMPARISON ........................................................ 161

BIBLIOGRAPHY....................................................................................... 163

ABOUT THE AUTHOR ............................................................................. 165

# Introduction

"I do not fix problems. I fix my thinking. Then problems fix themselves." — *Louise L. Hay*

From my colleagues' encounters to my own personal observations, the innumerable experiences in large-scale system architecture projects reveal that almost all failed or floundering projects have one thing in common: their system solution architecture is not clearly defined. The ambiguity, be it from requirements or solution ends, is attributed to poor architectural design originating from a lack of holistic thinking and murky architectural modeling. This prompted me to write this book on how to present enterprise solution system architecture with minimal complexity and uttermost clarity.

The thrust of the systematic thinking and modeling approach in this book is as follows:
— Simplicity-driven
  — Adopting a self-explanatory modeling framework and architectural philosophy.
  — Specifying *a minimal set of indispensable elements* by sticking to the KISS[1] principle, as simplicity is a powerful weapon to tackle architectural complexity.
  — Blurring strict metadata definitions with coarse-grained description and categorization.
— Holistic
  — Covering the *essence of enterprise architecture and solution architecture* from a broader perspective of *IT systems analysis*, ranging from IT strategic direction, enterprise capability, and business context to operational runtime.
  — Employing architecture overview (including pattern, reference architecture and

---

[1] Keep It Simple and Sensible (not the habitual "Stupid")

solution integration) to embody governing ideas and building blocks alongside cross-cutting relationship assurance.

- Enforcing *both structural and decisional architecture* by incorporating architectural guidance and metrics mapping into modeling work products.
- Pragmatic
  - Instilling concrete model elements with an *architectural thinking* process, based on years of IT experience in enterprise system architecture.
  - Following a realistic approach for easy solution landing.
  - Matching architectural elements to reality with cloud, virtual service, mobile devices, etc.
- IT Service-oriented
  - Categorizing four types of functional services, each possessing *unique characteristics* for task assignment and operational efficiency, especially for the design of servitization.
  - Introducing the elements of domain-oriented composite services to facilitate evolutionary architecture and *packaged service design.*
  - Maximizing IT services that can be automated and orchestrated in the system environment.
- Adaptable
  - Supporting both technical and domain dynamics under the most effective common denominator framework.
  - Including generic and drill-down elements, along with an optional set of elements for easy customization and extension.
  - Catering to both emergent architecture and intentional architecture for the sake of operational adaptability.

There are plenty of IT modeling frameworks and architectural design tools on the market today, including those for enterprise architecture (e.g., Enterprise Architect, and ArchiMate), software architecture (e.g., StarUML), agile architecture (e.g., Agile Testing Framework), and system solution architecture (e.g., Rational System Architect). They either create a feature of enterprise architecture (EA), RUP/UML-based software architecture, agile frameworks, or complex metadata modeling. This book contributes to *filling the gap* between EA/IT planning and software architecture, cutting out the fluff that some EA tools have while *not* delving into the detailed design of class/object level specifications. Experience shows that the right level of *abstraction* and *correlation* is conducive to architects in their enterprise solution planning, architectural design, and solution project environment.

This book's focus is not merely on application architecture, business architecture, or technical architecture, but on *holistic architecture*, accommodating most practical case scenarios. It also employs *agile thinking* for a flexible architectural framework, deviating from the conventional agile methodology and architecture standard.

| Caveats About this Book |
| --- |
| — This book is NOT intended for novices and requires a relevant IT architecture background. <br> — This book is created in color print. For the black-and-white version, you may reference the elements' color in the back cover. The diagram views shown in this book are crafted for architectural relevance, not for visual appeal or animation. <br> — This book focuses on the architectural solution's content, not the context (such as cost), although that is very important in solution project management. The context analysis in association with model properties is an extension of the modeling tool. |

# Chapter 1  A-ESA Framework

> "…the expert developers working on that project have a shared understanding of the system design. This shared understanding is called 'architecture.'" — *Martin Fowler*

Agile enterprise solution architecture (A-ESA) is a service-oriented IT architecture (hereinafter "architecture") for an enterprise-level IT system (hereinafter a "system") which, like the best-known IEEE[2] definition, concerns a *fundamental structure* of service components, their *relationships* to each other and to the environment, and the *principles* guiding its work product and evolution. *"An architecture is what is fundamental to a system – not necessarily everything about a system, but the essentials."* Architecture is about instituting a leading practice approach to solution design, it's not about fixing things.

The architecture model is a collection of concepts in the architectural context. It's an all-round framework for *a philosophical and reflective mindset*, with a shared understanding aimed at the following:

— Reaching common agreement on architectural integrity from *different viewpoints*[3]
— Managing complexity and working out the *right level of abstraction*
— Applying an *early verification and validation* to avoid costly mistakes later on
— Making the *right decisions* about various alternatives and understanding the impact of the changes
— Ensuring SLA[4] meets solution requirements and IT governance for *long-term quality assurance*

---

[2] Institute of Electrical and Electronics Engineers
[3] Viewpoint reflects the position of the subject in relation to the viewer.
[4] Service Level Agreement

— Producing *blueprints* for realization and implementation
— Facilitating IT *asset reuse* across organizations and reducing costs

Complex solution architecture without modeling, so to speak, resembles the blind men touching an elephant without a full set of perspectives. Architecting without the right modeling approach will not be effective in most cases. As an architecture model forms correlated *thinking blocks* and *building blocks* for further design work, the more complex and larger a system is, the more it becomes necessary to apply architecture models.

# 1.1 The Nature of IT Services

Traditionally, enterprise architecture and solution architecture work at diverse levels, with the former pinpointing the enterprise-level architecture building block (ABB) and the latter being the solution building block (SBB). Consequently, a great deal of solution deliverables are disconnected from the enterprise architecture deliverables.

The agile ESA[5] in this book provides a mechanism to connect enterprise architecture, solution architecture, and other architectures (business architecture, service architecture, etc.) to form a holistic view of the enterprise system via service modeling. Based on the Open Group's definition, *"a service is a logical representation of a repeatable activity that has a specified outcome."* Service is viewed largely as both a business and technical entity. It's self-contained and a *"black box"* for its consumers. Both business and technical professionals should communicate via a lingua franca of *service orientation* that is neither entirely business-centric nor technically oriented to bridge the gap between the enterprise and solution architecture, as well as between business and IT.

Agile ESA modeling uses *IT Service* as a core concept to generate architecture views. By general definition, a service utilizes a (formal or informal) contract between a consumer and a provider regarding the provision of the defined goods and services. An IT service is a service that requires IT automation. There are essentially three levels of IT services:

---

[5] ESA can also stand for Enterprise System Architecture

(1) service interaction (user interface and the like), (2) service offer (application, business, or data service), and (3) service system (technical service and infrastructure service). At the functional level (accentuated in this book), practical IT services can be categorized as follows: (1) interaction service, (2) application business logic service or process service, (3) data service, and (4) technical service. Arguably, IT services can be defined on different levels (see Table 1 for the variations and relevance).

| IT Service | Exemplar Definition Level | | |
|---|---|---|---|
| | EA-Ecosystem | Solution System | Functional |
| Service interaction | Act, performance or transaction | Application UI, use-case, line of automation | GUI[6] service |
| Service offer | Value proposition, catalog entry | Capability, service interface | Application logic service, process service, data service, technical service |
| Service system | Integrated resources, people, technology, money, information | Node, actor, system, etc. | Technical component |

Table 1: IT Service Levels

Slightly deviating from the IT4IT's definition and SOA[7] nomenclature, the IT service at the functional level in this book is principally composed of the following:
— Self-contained and relatively independent
— Decomposable and loosely coupled
— Functionally grouped in user interface, application business logic, data, and technical spaces
— Likely exposable through standard API[8] with either implicit or explicit interfaces

There are three levels of service connotation:
— *Service abstraction* (or *generalization*): a representation of a business capability or IT capability including application logic, data and technical services defined in the architectural context
— *Service interface*: service contract and API service
— *Service implementation*: service component and service configuration

---

[6] Graphical User Interface
[7] Service-oriented Architecture
[8] Application Programming Interface

*Service abstraction* is the core mission in an IT service-based architecture, as abstracted services impose a foundation on service interface and implementation. Meanwhile, these services clearly define business needs, IT applications, and technical constructs without specifying "how", allowing more agility and efficiency to embrace changes in policy, service contract, and service composition.

It's worth noting that the term service can take the form of more than one type of service, even within the IT context; for instance, service in the form of XaaS,[9] and service in the form of IT service management. Without belaboring the point, the IT service defined in this book concerns service-oriented architecture at an enterprise solution level, agnostic of the underlying technology. The IT service takes *multi-grained* forms, be it appservice, macroservice, microservice,[10] or miniservice, with coarse-grained service as the optimal focal point of interest.

# 1.2 Model Coverage and Intent

As seen from Figure 1, the agile ESA falls between enterprise architecture and solution architecture, leaning more toward the latter.

The agile enterprise solution architecture approach is primarily based on many leading practices in enterprise solution projects. It infers from more than a few architecture standards and specifications including well-known EA-level methodologies and frameworks (for example, Zachman, DoDAF,[11] TOGAF, MASA, [12] and SSADM [13]) and compares some specifications with ArchiMate (refer to Appendix V – ArchiMate Mapping).

While adopting a more straightforward framework and far fewer elements, agile

---

[9] X as a Service

[10] Microservice, as a collection of small autonomous services following the *Unix philosophy* of modularity and extensibility, models around a business domain with a self-contained and single business capability.

[11] Department of Defense Architecture Framework

[12] MASA (Mesh Application and Service Architecture), a modeling style by Gartner for digital transformation architecture.

[13] Structured Systems Analysis and Design Methodology

enterprise solution modeling incorporates extended architectural definitions, such as pattern views, metrics mapping, drill-down elements, and property specifications, all of which are easy to use from the practitioner's perspective. It applies to agile architectural style for the quick modeling of business architecture, application architecture, technical architecture, information architecture, integration architecture, operational architecture, security architecture, and so forth. The intermingling approach of connecting top-down capability and bottom-up service components makes the agile enterprise solution architecture practical and verifiable.

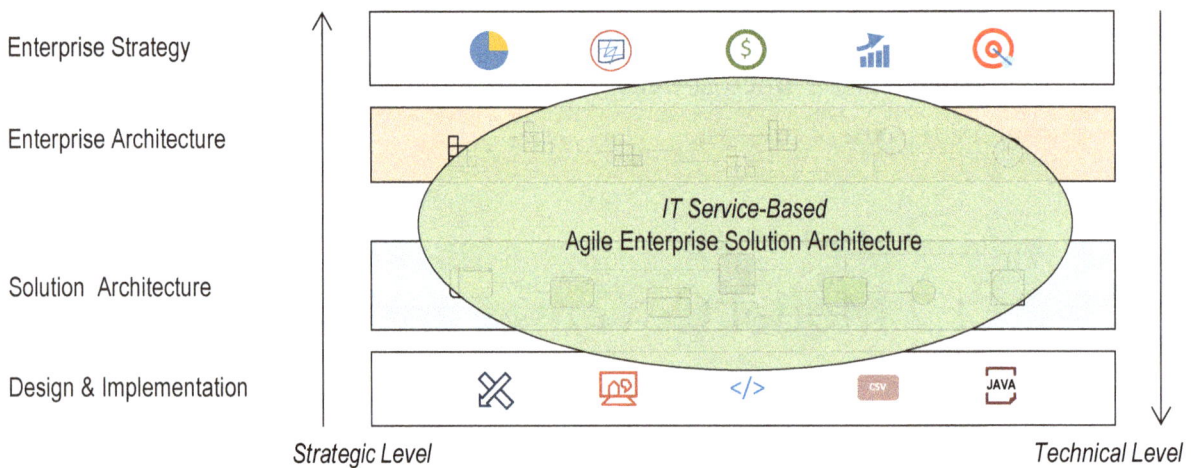

Figure 1: Agile ESA Coverage

The model is for chief architects, lead architects, and solutions architects to hammer out panoramic IT service views, and it stops at the service component interface level, with optional service component mapping. Component modeling and detailed object-level design are left to solution design architects such as software engineering architects, infrastructure architects, or designers who use various tools on the market in conformance with various standards, such as UMF, [14] the UML 4+1 View Model, and other process and data models.

With simplicity in mind, the model applies to a large audience: CTO, business analysts, project managers, consultants, developers, test specialists, and system administrators.

---

[14] Unified Method Framework

Due to the system architecture's nature, the modeling coverage does not spread to the financial and organizational aspects, though IT services are the basis for budgeting, cost estimation, timeline scheduling and ROI[15] analysis of the corporate IT plan. With a bit more wrap-around work, the modeling work products can also be presented to CEOs and business professionals as more straightforward IT planning than the traditional, high-level IT strategic plan.

# 1.3 Model Framework

*"Complexity is perplexing unless you know how to see."*
*— Thomas Vato*

The IT system model is analogous to building information modeling (BIM) or the three-view drawing in mechanical engineering, facilitated by AutoCAD drawing tools. Unlike building or mechanical modeling, the IT system is nebulous. One thing it has in common with modeling is its ability to connect the dots to produce the required plane views and establish three-dimensional models in an iterative and adaptive process. IT architecture via modeling connects dots from various viewpoints reflecting all stakeholder concerns and forms a rock-solid skeleton upon which a strong and desirable solution can be built.

This book's modeling conception is shown in Figure 2, where the IT system model starts from basic elements to yield views via a correlated relationship. Views from diverse viewpoints form a holistic architecture model (comprising of sectional models or partial models), representing IT systems consistently across the large solution landscape through a standard, yet reliable approach. An architecture view might be likened to a map, and a view to a model is what a map is to an atlas.

---

[15] Return of Investment

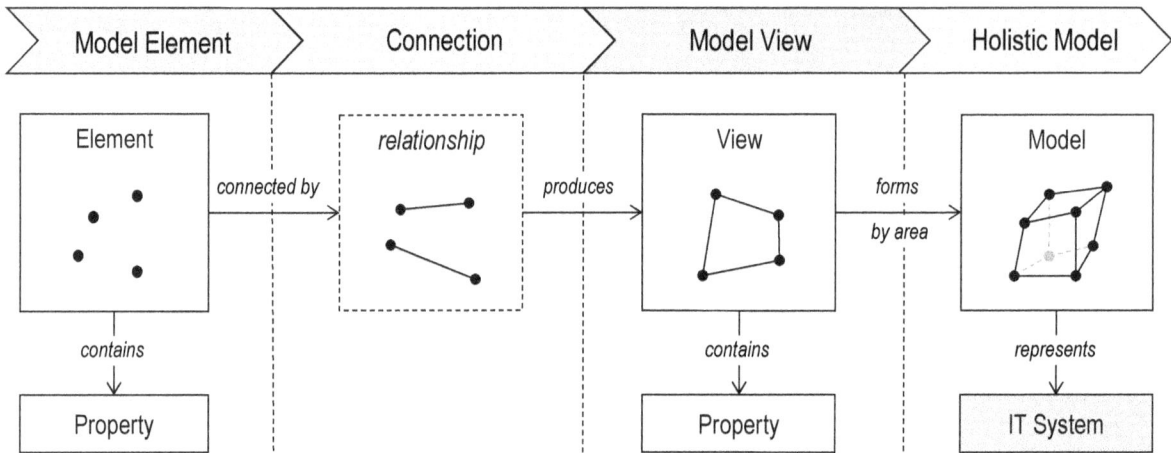

Figure 2: Basic ESA Modeling Conception

To facilitate the modeling process, views are grouped by *Aspect* (hereinafter referred to as an *Area* to avoid a discrepant definition). As shown in Figure 3, the simplified modeling framework representation encompasses five primary areas: (1) *Enterprise Capability Area*, (2) *Requirement Case Scenario Area*, (3) *Architecture Overview Area*, (4) *Functional Service Area*, and (5) *Infrastructural Area*. Of the five areas, the functional and infrastructural areas engender the landing blocks of the system model.

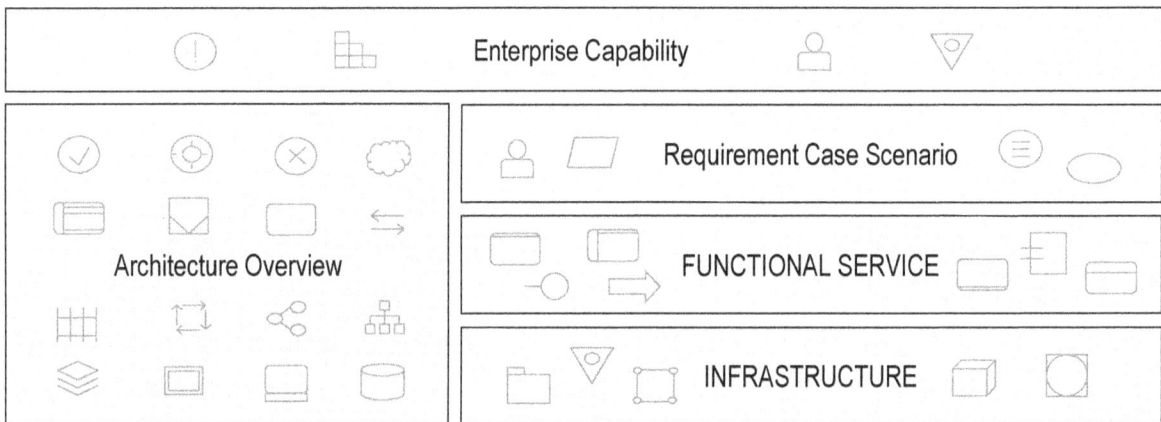

Figure 3: Areas of the Agile ESA Model

There are eleven fundamental views and four optional views associated with the model areas (Table 2). Each view contains elements and property attributes.

| Area | Fundamental View | Optional View |
|---|---|---|
| Capability | — Capability | — Organization |
| Case Scenario | — Use Case Model<br>— Process | — Page Flow |
| Architecture Overview | — Overview<br>— Pattern<br>— Metrics<br>— Relationship Validation | — DevOps |
| Function | — Interaction<br>— Relationship | — Service Component Realization |
| Infrastructure | — Deployment Package Mapping<br>— Deployment View | |

Note:
— *Architecture Overview Area* could have been subdivided into *Reference Pattern Area* and *Solution Validation Area*.
— *DevOps View* could have been categorized as part of *Pattern View*.
— The optional view is of assistance nature, supported by professionals other than architects.

Table 2: Agile ESA Model – Views

Essentially, the agile ESA modeling approach instills a systemic meta-thinking, together with Havruta[16]-style stakeholder partnership, that enforces solution assurance and architectural conformance, all of which intend to raise the *thinking ability*, and all the more so when it is endowed with purposeful views as *thinking maps.*

# 1.3.1 Model Area

Because an enterprise IT system (a system of systems) is very complex and large-scale, it's a tall order to express it in a panoramic model or in a single model view. The model area (or sectional model) refers to a part of the model views of particular concern to a stakeholder from a given viewpoint, conceivably through different perspectives.

Table 3 highlights the major concerns of each area, which organizes the views by key stakeholder groups (refer to Table 4 later).

.

---

[16] Somewhat heuristic questioning

| Area | Major Concerns | Note |
|---|---|---|
| Capability | Strategy, enterprise planning | |
| Requirement | User or system needs | |
| Overview | Architecturally significant concerns | Cross-cutting |
| Function | Application, data and technical services | |
| Infrastructure | Deployment and runtime | |

Table 3: Major Concerns of each Area

# 1.3.2 Model View

Almost all architects know the 4+1 View Model as well as the architecture description that conforms to the ISO/IEC 42010 standard. The Views and Viewpoints framework is generally defined as a part of the architecture standard that addresses a set of related concerns and is tailored to the specific stakeholders.

Figure 4 shows an agile ESA core framework adapted from the Views and Viewpoints. The *Stakeholder* has a concern addressed by the *Architecture View*, which is the central piece of an *Architecture Model*. The *Architecture View* represents the architecture model profiles, which account for the *Architectural Consideration* highlighted from the *Architecture Description*. The *Architecture View*, organized by *Architecture Area* (or *Architecture Aspect*), contains *Architecture Element* that forms the building blocks of the enterprise system solution architecture. Both view and element have *Property Specification* to represent key architectural considerations and architectural validation criteria.

For modeling simplicity, no emphasis is made on the dissimilarities among the view, viewpoint, and perspective as often termed in enterprise architecture.

Table 4 shows a list of commonly defined ESA views and their related stakeholders. In comparison with the model area, the view as an IT thinking block is a real visual representation of architectural modeling. It allows effective communication with all stakeholders, be they business or technical.

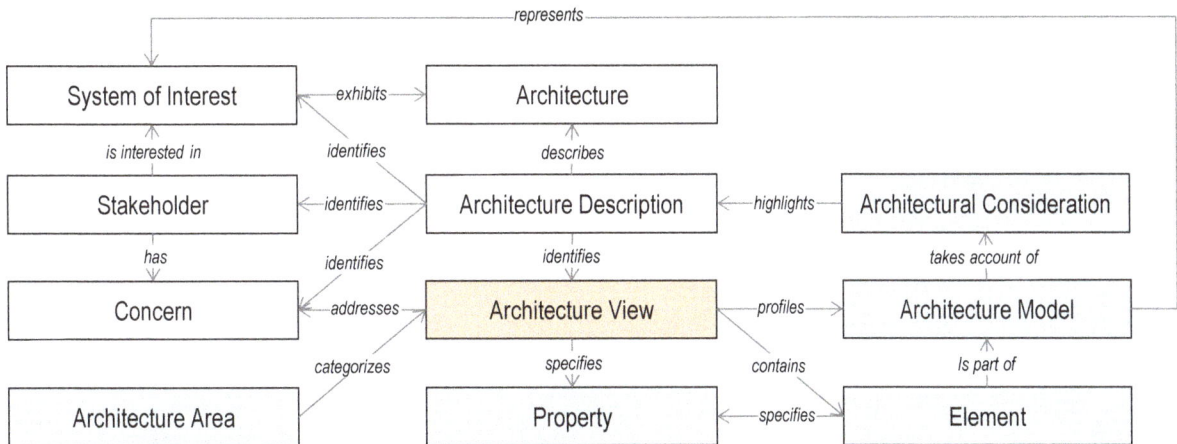

Figure 4: View as Centerpiece in the Conceptual Agile ESA

| Area | View | Abbr. | Primary/*Secondary* Stakeholder | |
|---|---|---|---|---|
| Enterprise | Capability | CAP | — CxO<br>— Strategy consultant<br>— Business analyst<br>— *Information architect*<br>— *Solution architect* | |
| | Organization (optional) | ORG | — Stakeholder | |
| Case Scenario | Use Case Model | UCM | — User | |
| | Process | PRM | — Business analyst<br>— Information architect<br>— Project manager<br>— Agile team<br>— *Solution architect*<br>— *UI team* | — BPM expert |
| | Page Flow View (optional) | PFV | — User<br>— Application architect<br>— Agile team<br>— *UI team*<br>— *Information architect* | |
| Function | Service Interaction | SIV | — User<br>— Application | — Application or systems |

| Area | View | Abbr. | Primary/*Secondary* Stakeholder | |
|---|---|---|---|---|
| | | | architect | programmer |
| | Service Relationship | SRV | — Solution architect<br>— Designer | — Development lead<br>— Information architect |
| | Service Component Realization (optional) | SCR | — Solution architect<br>— Developer | |
| Infrastructure | Package Mapping | DPM | — Solution architect | — Application architect<br>— Integration architect<br>— Operational architect |
| | Deployment View | DEP | | — Infrastructure architect |
| Architecture Overview | Overview | AOV | — Chief or lead architect<br>— Solution architect | — *Domain guru* |
| | Pattern | PTN | | — Method expert |
| | Metrics | MTS | | |
| | DevOps (optional) | DEV | | — Development lead<br>— Operational architect<br>— Systems admin |
| | Relationship Validation | VLD | — Chief or lead architect<br>— Solution architect<br>— User | |
| Note:<br>— The *italic* indicates the secondary stakeholders. | | | | |

Table 4: Commonly Defined Views and their Stakeholders

# 1.3.2.1 Correlation View vs. Sketch View

There are two kinds of views in terms of element correlation:

— *Correlated view or model view*: Its elements are correlated to each other in the model.

— *Sketch view or draft view*: Its elements are for reference and pattern usage, not directly correlated to other elements in the model, and will not be shown in a relationship view other than its own view (commonly referred to as *diagram*).

As is often the case, conceptual views primarily come into play for a green-field architectural design. The conceptual views are the views of exploration. In the A-ESA model, the sketch views belong to the conceptual views. Their elements are not required to be correlated in the solution architectural context.

While a model view must be correlated and traceable, a view for presentation or communication can take the form of both a correlated view and a sketch view. For example, a pattern view can either be a correlated view when it's part of the solution element or a sketch view when it's part of the reference architecture or a draft diagram. Table 5 shows the nature of each presentation view within this book in terms of correlation.

| Area | View | Correlated | Sketch |
|---|---|---|---|
| Enterprise | Capability | x | |
| | Organization | x | |
| Case Scenario | Use Case Model | x | |
| | Process | x | |
| | Page Flow | x | |
| Architecture Overview | Overview | x | x |
| | Pattern | x | x |
| | Metrics | x | |
| | DevOps | x | x |
| | Cross-checking Relationship | x | |
| Function | Service Interaction | x | |
| | Service Relationship | x | |
| | Service Component Realization | x | x |
| Infrastructure | Package Mapping | x | |
| | Deployment View | x | |

Table 5: Correlated View and Sketch View

# 1.3.2.2 Logical View vs. Physical View

The logical view guides the architectural design. The physical view expresses how the structure would be architecturally realized or built. The logical views tend to be generic and more reusable, while the physical views display middleware products or implemented components.

# 1.3.3 Model Element

The element is the fundamental part of the agile ESA model. All model view elements should be correlated, following the coarsely defined metadata model. Figure 5 presents an overview of the core elements and their relationships, where elements are grouped by layer for ease of comprehension.

At the enterprise strategic level:
— the *Principle* impacts the *Capability* and serves as a guide to the *Key Architectural Consideration*
— the *Capability* profiles the functions or processes of the enterprise system

At the business requirement level:
— the *Role* acts upon the *Use Case* and the *Process Task*
— the *Requirement* is formalized by the *Use Case*
— the *Task* is automated via the *Use Case* specification

At the architecture overview level:
— the *Generic Service* or *Domain* generalizes and groups IT services
— the *Key Choice (or Key Consideration)* determines the system solution's shape and substance, from the *Requirement* input, the *Principle* guideline, and the *Governance*

At the functional level:
— the *User Interface* element takes input from the presentation layer, and invokes the *Application Logic Service*
— the *Application Logic Service* takes control of business flows and action events and invokes the *Technical Service* and/or the *Data Service*
— the *Technical Service* invokes the *Data Service* if any, and performs tasks independent of the *Application Logic Service*
— the *Data Service* provides data content, either from a single source or from aggregated, consolidated, or federated sources
— the *Service Interface* exposes application programming interfaces originating from the *Service Component* and acts as a service provider from any of the exposed IT services

— the *Service Component,* not the model's focal, is deployed into the *Package* based on the required service-level characteristics of the system

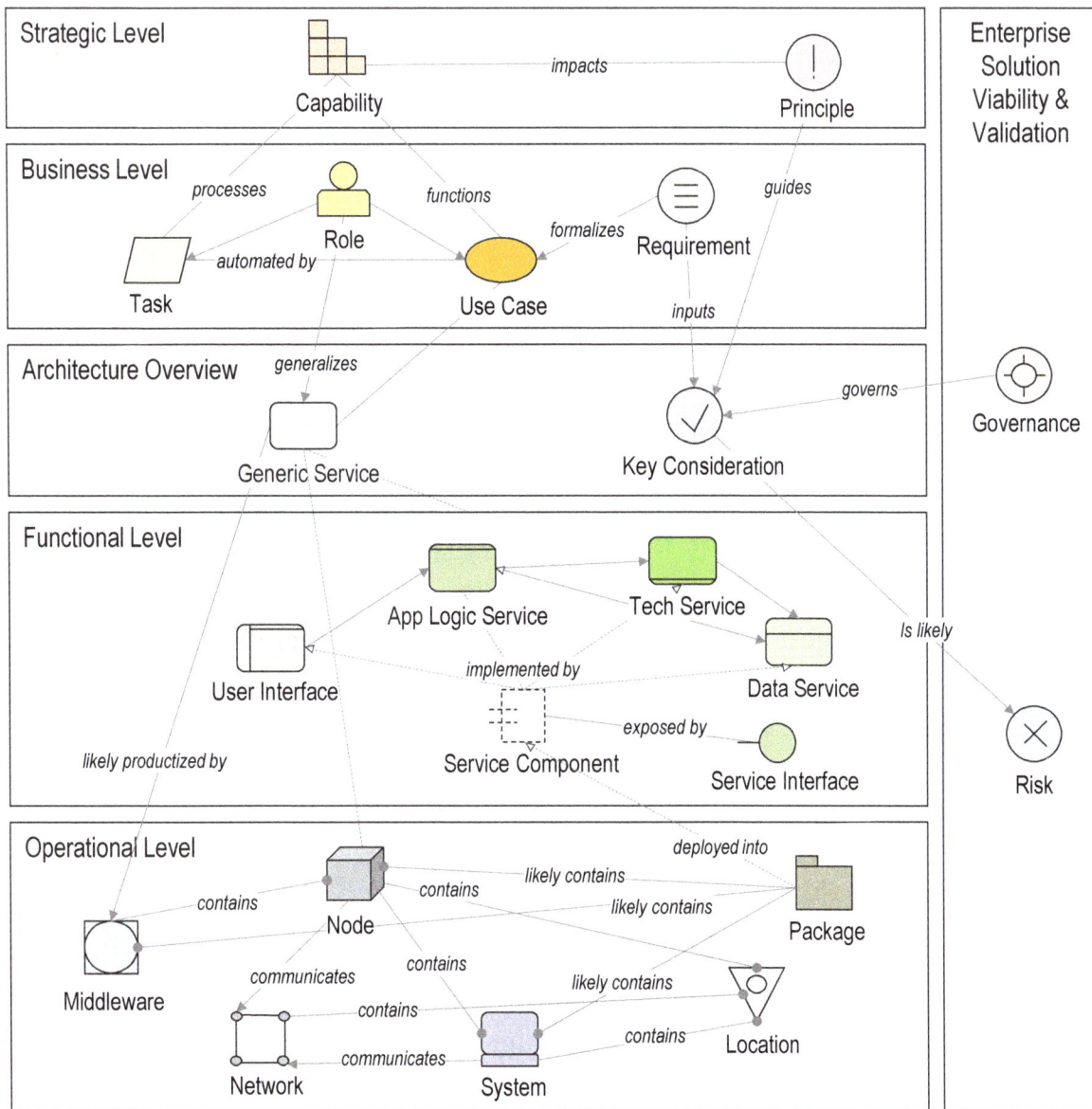

Figure 5: Overview of Core Elements and Relationships

At the infrastructure and operational runtime level:

— the *Package* is deployed onto the *Container,* part of the *Node* construct
— the *Node* primarily executes the *Middleware* and the *Package*
— the *Location* primarily contains the *Node,* the *Network,* and the *System*

— the *System* is normally built on its own node, and likely contains the *Package* element

— the *Middleware* is situated on the *Node*, and likely contains the *Deployed Package*

— the *Network*, as a communication means, connects the *Node*, the *System,* and the like

At the enterprise solution validation level:

— the *Governance* validates the *Key Choice*

— the *Risk* logs potential issues that need to be addressed and resolved, somewhat beyond the scope of architect's sole responsibilities

By applying *an identical set of architectural elements*, various stakeholders can gain a common understanding of the functional domains and system architecture. Chapter 3 gives a brief description of each element. Appendix III shows a complete list of model elements.

# 1.3.4 Model Property

Both view and element constitute properties (or attributes) that reflect various enterprise and architectural concerns as part of the architectural thinking process. Property attributes can be customized or extended to fit changing environments and embody emergent system characteristics. Depending on the profile specifications for each solution, they can be inherited or inferred, displayed explicitly, implicitly, or selectively.

The property attributes are deceptively simple, yet considerably meaningful. Regardless, this book does not elaborate on the properties. Example property specifications can be seen from the walkthrough case study in Chapter 4.

# 1.4 Modeling for Change

Agile is a *mindset* that drives architectural design. Agile architecture shifts from experience-based to *fact-based decision-making*. Whether adopting an open-source or feature-driven approach in an agile digital enterprise environment, *continuous architecture* (or MVAM[17]) plays a vital role in avoiding *spaghetti designs* leading to *architectural debts*. Enterprise solution architecture constitutes the key to success for agile teams (either feature or component teams). A parochial view of the so-called guerrilla-style agile architecture may work occasionally. Nevertheless, it can lead to disasters — as the cold reality tells us, most systems co-exist with several or even hundreds of other systems. A walkthrough diagnostic of the holistic solution model can help identify potential issues.

Agile modeling particularly applies to the system environment that is volatile and subject to change, and it allows for it to be understood and explored quickly. To be proficient in terms of agility means to be proficient at managing change. More broadly, agile modeling is not limited merely to product-centric agile architecture. Agile architecture requires simpler, more holistic architectural modeling, as complex modeling is only narrowly subject to change. Even as IT modeling becomes more automated via AI, IT architecture will still be required to construct reusable building blocks at different layers of abstraction and facilitate understanding among stakeholders. It should be taken into account that the significance of architecture is sized up by the *cost of change*. Not all change can or should be anticipated. As requirements change, well-modeled architecture should not be reduced to an *endless cycle of iterations*.

IT architecture is *both an art and a science*, which requires the flexible use of modeling. For complete project thoughtfulness, the model *Areas* or *Views* concerning stakeholder viewpoints need to be explored first. Keep in mind that you shouldn't wait until all capabilities and/or requirements are in place. Beware of ivory-tower architecture or the waterfall approach that is unproven and unrealistic. Architectural modeling is an iterative process; a see-saw process that leads to a proper tradeoff balance in the end. Start small and build up the idealized form over time. Apply the principle of jaggedness to fit each solution environment and adopt the *right-level approach* to agile modeling. Focus on the *architecturally significant requirement scenarios* and solution needs. Essentially, modeling facilitates requirement mapping and IT-solution thinking. Solution modeling is anything but simple and may be fairly time-consuming, however,

---

[17] Minimum Viable Architecture Model, the least/smallest architecture

it's rewarded a thousand-fold in the long term.

The modeling technique is primarily applicable to self-adapting complex system architecture, as simple architecture does not warrant the same amount of time and effort. Unlike building architecture, most system architecture (particularly systems of engagement) is evidently subject to change. To manage the *complexity around change*, several guidelines are recommended:

— Architect for purpose: don't plan too far ahead; otherwise, waste resources or commit unrealistic goals.
— Employ proven design patterns: use leading practices or reference architectures whenever possible.
— Use a system-of-systems approach if necessary, and present coarse-grained services.
— Leverage the domain-level elements: generalize or group services and form a sub-view to reduce illegibility and complexity.
— Divide and conquer: employ partitions, especially layering techniques, to distinguish services of similar responsibilities or certain characteristics.
— Apply abstraction or generalization: elevate details to the architectural level, commonly known as the black-box approach.
— Adopt AI-powered tools: create more concrete system architecture models using automation tooling.

In short, just like software needs robust documentation to be maintained, architecture needs a sound modeling methodology. Agile modeling ensures that models are incrementally created, easy to follow, sufficiently accurate, consistent, and adaptable.

# Chapter 2  A-ESA Areas and Views

"Everything should be made as simple as possible, but not simpler."
— *Albert Einstein*

This chapter is a brief description of the agile ESA architecture's *Areas* and *Views*. The initial choice of areas and views in a solution architecture depends on the entry point(s) of the project's nature and scope. As good solution modeling only addresses significant concerns, the model areas and views are targeted to tackle complexity and scale issues based on importance, urgency, budget, and effort rather than being fully fledged.

# 2.1 Enterprise Area

The *Enterprise Area* (or *Enterprise Capability Area*) covers enterprise architecture capability, business service capability, and IT resource capability. It blurs the demarcation between enterprise architecture (EA) capability, business architecture, and capability requirements while serving as a strategic point for heat map analysis, ROI analysis, and enterprise planning.

Note that the *Enterprise Area* covers all capabilities in an enterprise, but the enterprise system solution architecture is generally concerned with the related IT system capabilities within the scope (that is, the capabilities that need to be automated due to the case scenario requirements).

# 2.1.1 Capability View

*Capability View* provides a categorization and rationalization of capabilities. The categories normally have no more than three or four levels, beyond which it is plausibly too granular. *Capability View* can include a dynamic analysis of interaction and dependency among capabilities in addition to the common capability taxonomy in block format. Each capability can be regarded as an abstracted building block and identifies a *unique owner*. Capabilities specify *a cohesive set of accountabilities or resources* that a service (provided by one or more participants) might offer.

The lowest level of capability is associated with services or products. The services in association with the lowest level of capability in the *Capability View* give an initial service portfolio, and detailed mapping occurs in the solution architecture's functional area. The mapped services and offering services will likely be contained in the service repository for API management.

*Capability View* can reference the CBM[18] approach, in which each capability is assigned one of the three levels (direct, control, and execute). In practice, though, capabilities are ordinarily grouped by layered domains.

The *Capability Model*, covering all enterprise capabilities, can be convoluted in terms of the overlapping nature of the categorization structure. Sometimes, it's initially categorized through a Tree Map or MECE[19] analysis.

The *Capability View* can be a powerful tool for ITSP[20] as seen in the following examples:
— *IT coverage rate* (IT-enabled capabilities divided by all capabilities) signals an enterprise's informationization.
— *Capability relationship mapping*, together with value stream analysis, helps form a meaningful *capability ontology* for heat-map identification and KPI targeting.

Traditionally, the *Capability Model* has an association with the Business Activity Model, the Business Role Model, and the Enterprise Information Model, and ultimately the

---

[18] Component Business Model
[19] Mutually Exclusive Collectively Exhaustive
[20] IT Strategic Plan

Business Structure Model. In this book, all of these are simplified into *Capability View* encapsulating various services driven by case scenarios. Remember, enabling agility through the conceptualization of IT capabilities is the focal point of agile architecture. *Capability-centric architecture* at the operating model level is more suitable for microservices than a more traditional data-centric architecture.

The illustration below (Figure 6) demonstrates the *Capability View* of a major business domain.

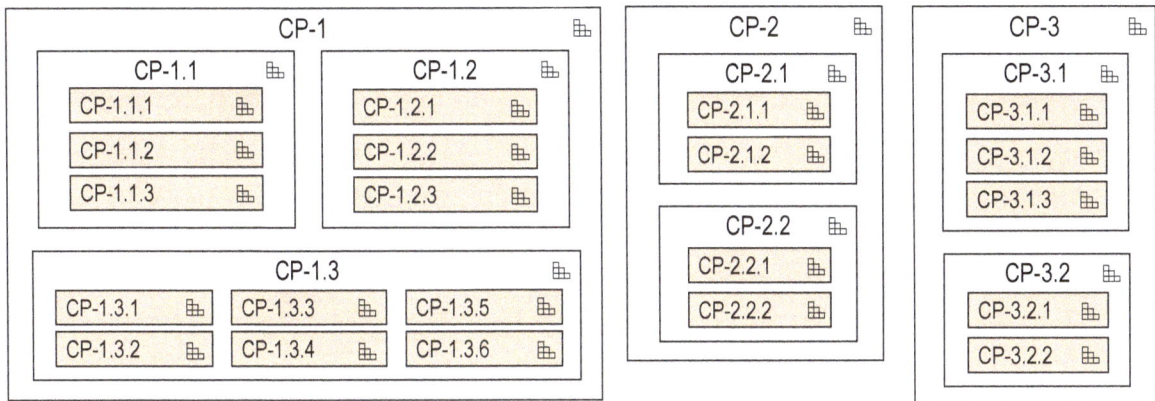

Figure 6: Illustration of Capability View

# 2.1.2 Organization View

Organization plays a key role in a system solution, given that plenty of issues are organizational issues. Per Conway's law, the structure of a system always mirrors the structure of the organization that created it.

*Organization View* can be an optional view similar to a traditional organization chart, but it's a must in some cases. For instance, in a DevOps[21] environment, the organization structure needs to be clarified before the development teams become effective. Similarly, when using *Process View*, the role relationship information from *Organization View* is

---

[21] Development and Operations

helpful for human task assignments.

The *Role Element*, loosely defined in the model, can refer to both stakeholder and user type in the organizational context. Hence, it can be a liaison between business and IT as a stakeholder or a touch-point to the system as a user.

# 2.2 Case Scenario Area

The *Case Scenario Area* is also called the *Requirement Case Scenario Area*, recording all customer requirements and inferred value propositions for the solution. It's noteworthy that requirement case scenario not only expresses what customers want but also their *implicit requirement concerns.* Just a saying goes, there's more to it than meets the eye.

The case scenario associates with enterprise capability to a great extent. As seen in Figure 7, the capability and the case scenario lead to the same result (in most cases matched, though not always). Generally, *Use Case* and *Sub Process* are candidate IT service, atomic, or composite service.

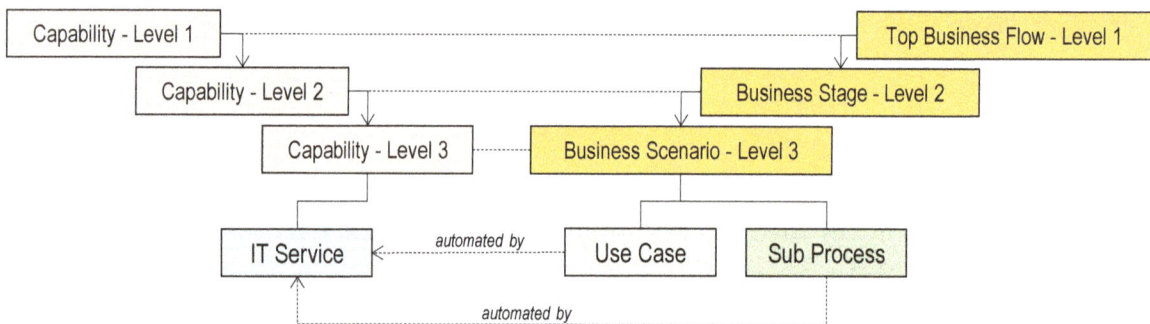

Figure 7: Capability vs. Case Scenario

For an agile case scenario gathering, it's helpful to use the *design thinking* framework (a human-centered approach to architecture) together with the system thinking later on.

# 2.2.1 Use Case Model View

Traditionally, use-cases define interactions between external actors and the system to achieve particular goals. Let's take a look at several use-case examples from order management:

— Create a new order
— Search catalog
— Work with shopping lists
— Update order
— Cancel order
— Change delivery slot

The Use Case Model (UCM) is nothing new; it's a group of related use-cases expressed in a bubble shape. The *UCM View* (see Figure 8) is a simplified portrayal illustrating how actors and external systems interact with the solution system without stereotypical definitions. It clearly defines a boundary, a thoughtful sub-system context, business context, or domain scope.

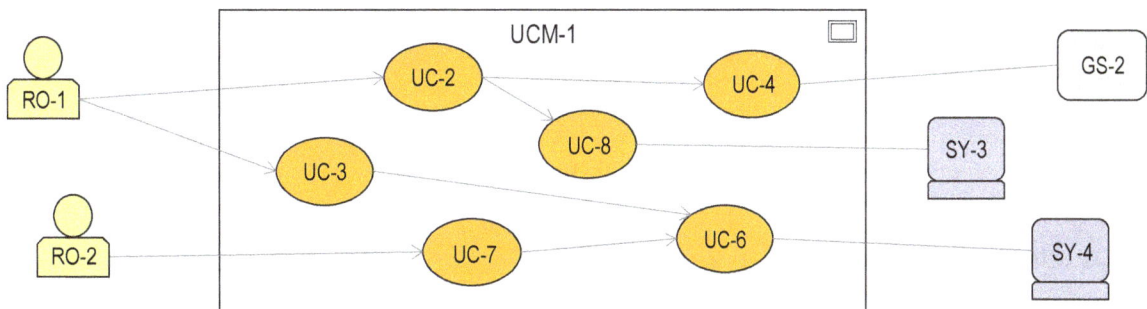

Figure 8: Illustration of Use Case Model

Please note that agile case requirement gathering uses different UX[22] techniques, including User Journey Map, Features, Epic, and User Story[23] along with User Profile and Personas, or even Event Storming. However, in many cases, for clearer requirement

---

[22] User Experience
[23] User Story normally takes the form of [ user | action | benefit ].

correlation and crucial dependency mapping (tracking down to the system functionality), *UCM View* or *Use Case View* (preferably in a simplified form) is still recommended. Keep in mind: *the value of modeling extends way beyond simple visualization.*

## 2.2.2 Process View

*Process View* illustrates a collection of linked tasks that deliver a client's service or product to accomplish an organizational goal. It adopts a simple process-modeling approach for easy understanding without a smattering of BPMN,[24] to say nothing of BPEL.[25] Figure 9 illustrates the *Process View*.

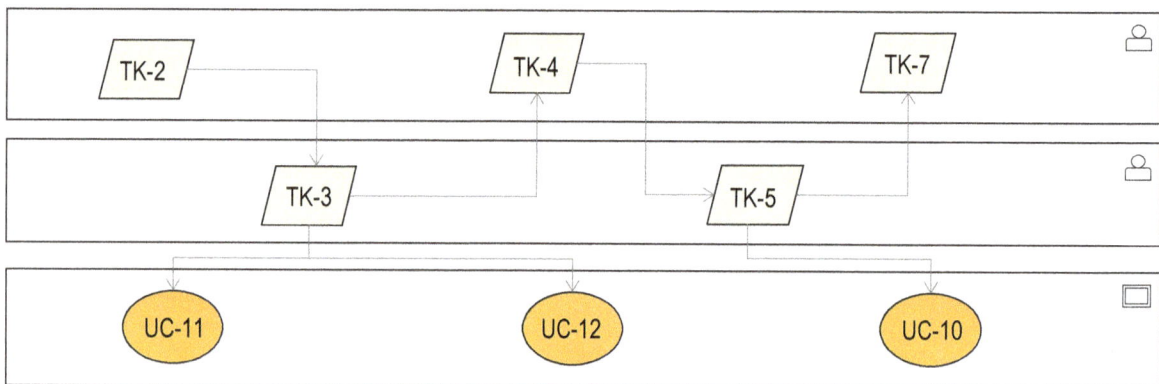

Figure 9: Illustration of Process View

Special attention needs to be given to the flows across human and machine boundaries that represent the functional requirements placed on the IT system. This view is featured by modeling the *line of automation* (processing) and *digitization* (data).

In a complex business scenario, there are layers of processes for modeling. Figure 10 shows the layered process taxonomy, typically seen in a functional organization. When opting for products or services that cross multiple functions, a similar layered process approach using value-stream visual maps can be applied instead. Note that tasks stand

---

[24] Business Process Model and Notation
[25] Business Process Execution Language

for value-adding activities instead of time-ordered tasks in a value-stream process.

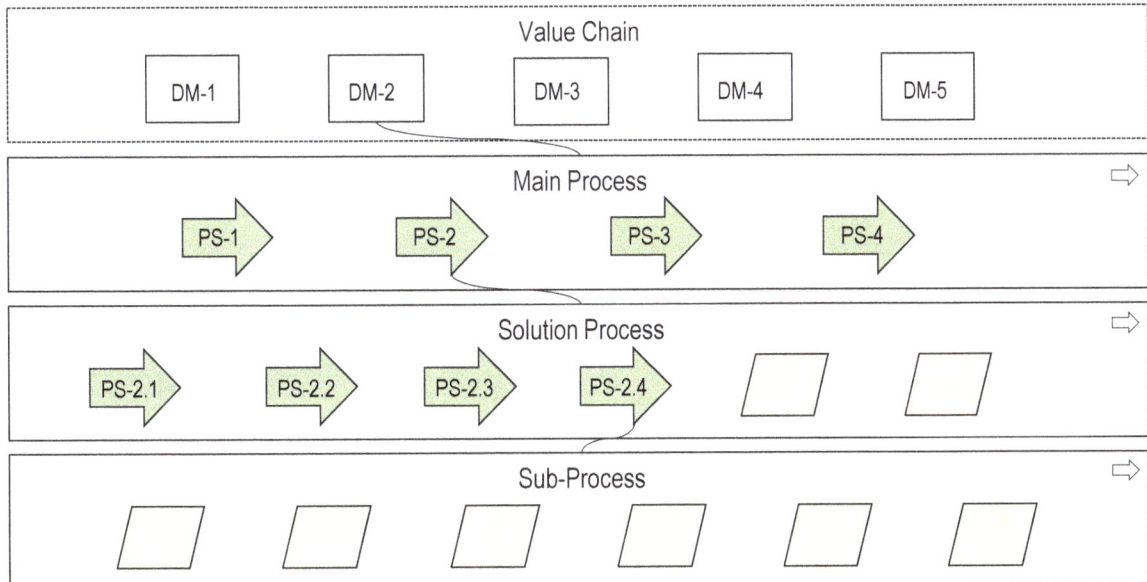

Figure 10: Layered Process Taxonomy

The information contained in a process flow or tasks requires an examination of the underlying data structure and relationship. An initial ERD[26] may help. This view may contain more details about process objectives, activity specifications and dynamics, input and output, role, rule, data and other resources.

Note that *Process View* can be used for strategic planning or business architecture, for example, when combining value stream analysis and capability cross-mapping.

# 2.2.3 Page Flow View

*Page Flow View* is a series of graphical user interface representations often rendered in sketch diagrams that express requirements more intuitively. It's extremely useful in real-world scenarios, especially user-centered design approaches. Figure 11 illustrates

---

[26] Entity Relationship Diagram

*Page Flow View*, including the extension element <<screen>>.

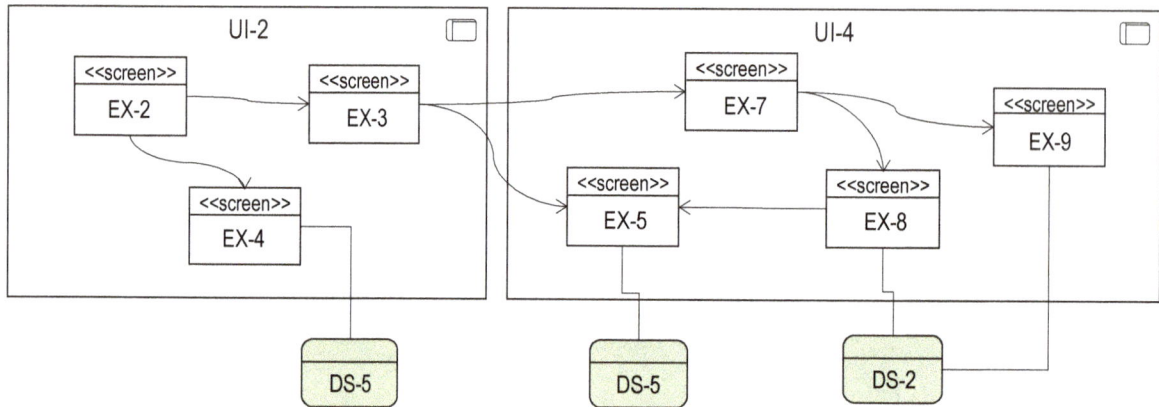

Figure 11: Illustration of Page Flow View

Your knee-jerk reaction to the *Page Flow View* might be: is it really so simple? It seems so. The *Page Flow View* is not intended to be a graphic user interface design chart; rather, it gives *guidance for GUI design* and an association with the GUI services into which the <<screen>> can be incorporated. Notably, *Page Flow View* is mainly used for overall system architecture thoughtfulness relating to non-functional requirements, especially usability and multi-experience, but there's a catch. It's *not* for application design in software engineering, so the detailed layout and visual appeal aren't a concern.

It should be noted that in the Use Case Model or Domain Model, the screen and GUI elements are normally not included.

# 2.3 Architecture Overview Area

The *Architecture Overview (AO) Area* covers the overall pictures of the enterprise system. It stresses top-level architectural constructs, represented in either a *Tier View*, *Layer View*, or *Sketch View*. This area also includes *Pattern View* (framework, reference architecture, enterprise design pattern, asset, and leading practice) for governing ideas, *Metrics View* for critical decision-making, and an optional *DevOps View* for continuous development and deployment. It's typically presented as a cross-cutting solution view, useful for scenarios such as a *Big Data Solution View* ranging from the application to the platform.

The solution-level architecture overview is part of the enterprise architecture landscape and reflects the enterprise capabilities related to the solution. The *AO Area* can embody multiple solutions at an enterprise architecture level and virtually encompass all elements. In reality, certain architectural issues can only be understood as a whole.

# 2.3.1 Outline View

The *Architecture Outline View,* or habitually *Architecture Overview* (including enterprise overview, conceptual overview, and solution overview), is the most flexible view, allowing both a correlated view and a sketch view. The *AO View* can take distinctive forms and run through different perspectives (application, technical, logical, physical, functional or infrastructural). It also contains a well-defined system context and covers both as-is and to-be IT environments.

It's worth mentioning that an architecture overview can cater to a specific audience and be subject to changing requirements. The *AO View* reflects common viewpoints for consensus discussion with its audience: In practice, it primarily takes the form of an enterprise business overview, IT system overview, service layer overview, and application platform overview to address major architectural concerns.

# 2.3.1.1 Layer View

*Layer View* normally exemplifies the overall architecture's *governing ideas*, with *building blocks* showing functionalities, capabilities, resources, middleware, etc. It can portray structural break-down, layering, high-level grouping, building-blocks' relationship, and much more (see the illustration in Figure 12).

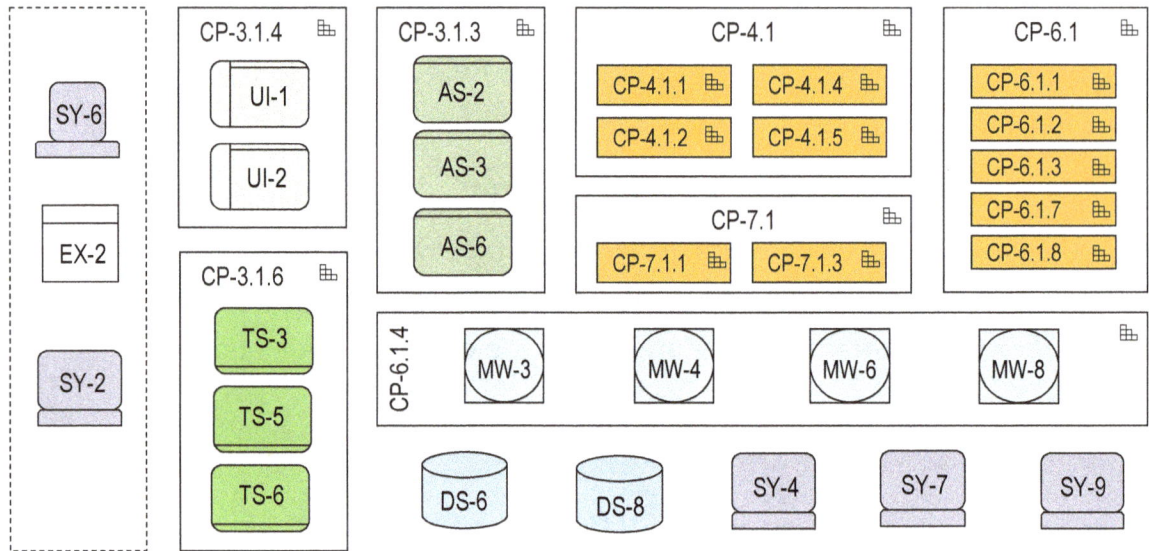

Figure 12: Illustration of Architecture Block View

## 2.3.1.2 Tier View

*Tier View* is a prominent view for overall solution landing. The view is typically divided by tier (see Figure 13), a physical distribution different from the layer's logical division. In practice, the physical tier is often referred to as two-tier, three-tier, and n-tier architecture.

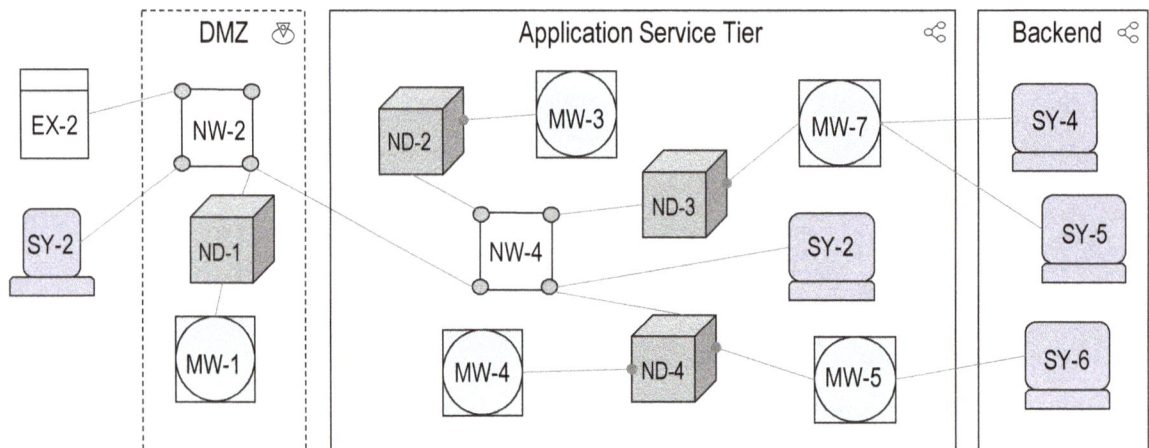

Figure 13: Illustration of Architecture Tier View

## 2.3.1.3 Sketch View

*Sketch View* is typically a conceptual view, or an *informal diagram*, showing the initial ideas of the innovative solution or overall architecture, without strict element mapping. Example sketch views also include gap assessment, business context, and IT environment.

## 2.3.1.4 System Context View

As its name suggests, the *System Context View* defines the boundary between the solution system and the key external systems, entities, actors, and interfaces, along with the often-required specification of major *information flow* (requested info) and *control flow* (such as communication access protocol, frequency, and volume). Figure 14 demonstrates the *System Context View*.

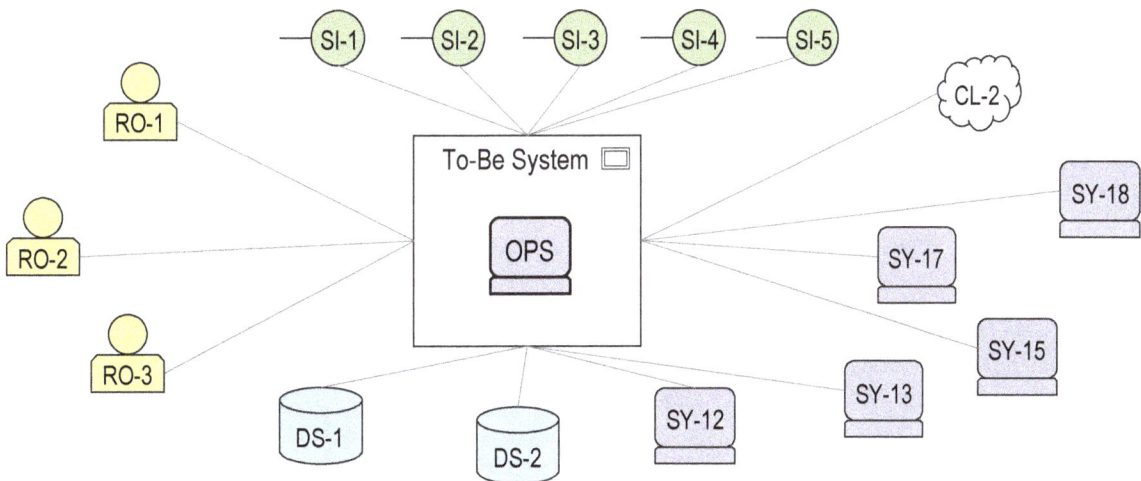

Figure 14: Illustration of System Context View

Essentially, the *System Context View* defines the enterprise solution scope and reflects its profile or building block(s) from its upper-level enterprise architecture.

In contrast to the *System Context View*, the *Business Context View* expresses how enterprise and organizational entities relate to each other through information exchange. However, it does not distinguish between the various users and actors, and it does not generally represent the to-be application system platform. Consequently, the *Business Context View* is not regarded as a required IT model view.

# 2.3.2 Pattern View

"The best architectures are full of patterns." — *Grady Booch*

An architecture pattern archetypally represents well-structured operational collaborations between IT services. It's an extraordinary value of IT service-based solutions. *Pattern View* can be either a correlated model view or a sketch view. It's mostly borrowed from leading practices and tailored for the intended solutions. The *Pattern View* addresses architectural concerns and has a wide range of coverage, such as Migration View, Business Pattern View, Analytics Design View, and Integration View. *Integration View*, for instance, can be a signboard of various integration styles: UI collaboration, data federation or distribution, message-oriented enterprise bus, service-oriented orchestration, security integration, and API-centric agile integration. Figure 15 demonstrates an example of a *Pattern View* containing the cloud platform services.

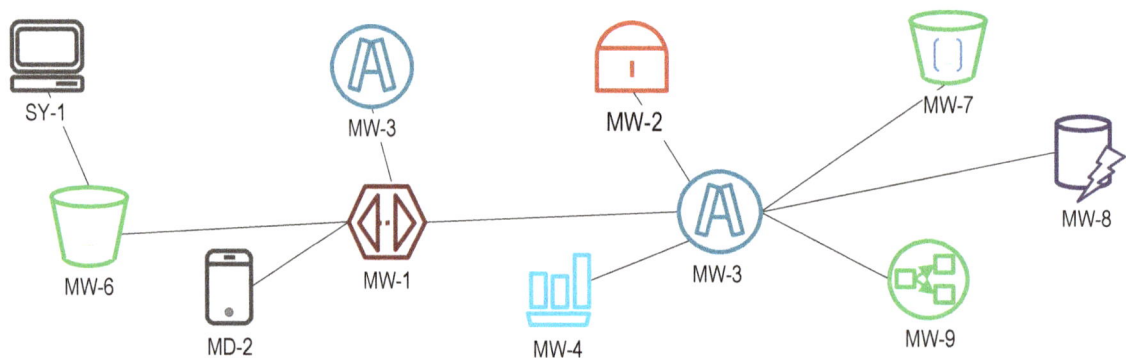

Figure 15: Illustration of Pattern View

# 2.3.3 Metrics View

"Decision making is there where complexity and simplicity meet."
— *Jos Berkemeijer*

*Metrics View*, part of the architecture overview, is unique and the most vital view and thinking framework for architectural contemplations. Its simple mapping aids decision-making theatrically in a complex solution environment. Unlike structural modeling, *Metrics View* explores what matters most from a *decisional school of thought*.

The term *Metrics* is loosely defined for simplified categorization. An architect can visually identify the architectural emphasis, innovative points, and challenging roadblocks by placing all key metrics in this view and reflecting a full-scale viewpoint, from the business requirements and enterprise architecture to solution architecture, and project management (peripherally). It's a cross-cutting view covering both requirement and solution perspectives. The metrics elements can also be displayed in other model views to highlight their architectural significance. Figure 16 illustrates the *Metrics View* for an initial solution architecture phase.

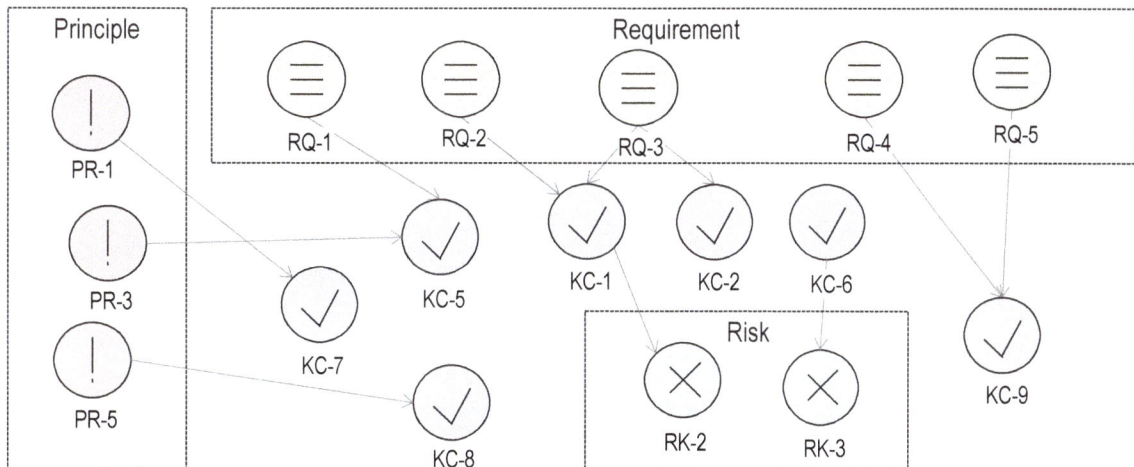

Figure 16: Illustration of Metrics View

Input elements for the metrics view are principle, requirement (functional, non-functional, and rule), and governance elements. They can also map to the *View Frame Element* for an already-chosen decision. Output elements are the key choice (the crucial metrics element) and risk elements. See Chapter 3 – Table 9 for clear source mapping.

All elements in *Metrics View* need to be mapped at least once. If not, the unmapped element will be flagged as unrelated, unjustified, or unrealizable. The unmatched element will be shown in a highlight as a reminder.

# 2.3.4 DevOps View

*DevOps View*, covering both functional and infrastructural areas, fits agile or evolutionary architecture for continuous development and deployment. It helps layout the DevOps environment, indirectly associated with the enterprise organization structure. The DevOps platform physically belongs to the *Infrastructural Area*.

A few points need to be kept in mind regarding DevOps:
— DevOps fits well in a *cloud-native digital platform* environment. It's a natural choice for an iterative MVP[27] architectural approach, but it's not a must for some other solution architectures, say, big up-front design system architecture.
— DevOps varies to different degrees. For example, it can become DevSecOps where security is ingrained in the full software delivery lifecycle.
— DevOps involves people, culture, and processes, not merely a technology platform or tools.

# 2.3.5 Relationship Validation View

*Relationship Validation View* is usually generated automatically from tools, however manual changes are recommended to correct certain structural inconsistency and

---

[27] Minimal Viable Product

decisional misbehavior.

*Relationship Validation View* covers a large number of snapshot views, such as:
— Application service relationship snapshot
— Data service relationship snapshot
— Technical service relationship snapshot
— DevOps chain relationship snapshot
— Middleware relationship snapshot
— Network relationship snapshot
— Node relationship snapshot
— System relationship snapshot
— Application and data service relationship snapshot
— Application and technical service relationship snapshot
— Application, data and technical service relationship snapshot
— Application, data, technical service and system relationship snapshot
— And so on and so forth

*Relationship Validation View* helps check the following concerns:
— Are all relationships connected correctly?
— What's missing, and will it have a significant impact?
— Are the core interfaces well-defined and interoperable?
— Are all the services defined well in the coupling, layering, granularity, integration, and isolation?
— Have all the key non-functional requirements been walked through?
— Is there any risk that will become an issue? If so, what's the architectural alternative?
— Is any estimation, simulation, or testing necessary?

*Relationship Validation View* provides a holistic inspection of views and elements for cross-cutting consistency and issue detection. More importantly, the *Relationship Validation View* can also display an invoking chain relationship for various case scenarios, identifying potential hot spots or bottlenecks for red-flag alerts, and show various statistics. This makes the solution architecture more measurable and manageable, resulting in a robust solution system.

With tooling support, many of the validation tasks can be performed automatically. For example, in the operational *Deployment View*, by applying the least cost routing/minimal spanning tree algorithm based on the Dijkstra algorithm, the routed connections will be automatically derived.

## 2.3.5.1 Property Validation View

*Property Validation View* shows which required properties are not minimally specified or validated. It also shows various statistics for solution completeness, architectural estimation, and task scheduling.

## 2.3.5.2 Matrix Validation View

*Matrix View* demonstrates various relationships in a tabular form, including relationship matrices and usage statistics. For example, the *Relationship Matrix View* can display technical transaction mappings and usage statistics, showing how many GUI services, technical services, or data services are related to an application logic service. Figure 17 illustrates an example of *Deployment Package Mapping Matrix View*.

|  | UI-2 | AS-2 | AS-5 | TS-2 | TS-4 | TS-7 | TS-8 | DS-4 | DS-6 | DS-3 | UI-1 | TS-5 | TS-3 | DS-7 | DS-8 |
|---|---|---|---|---|---|---|---|---|---|---|---|---|---|---|---|
| DP-1 | X |  |  |  |  | X |  |  |  |  | X |  |  |  |  |
| DP-2 |  |  |  | X |  | X | X |  |  |  |  |  | X |  | X |
| DP-3 |  | X | X |  | X |  | X |  |  |  |  | X |  | X |  |
| DP-4 |  |  |  |  |  |  |  | X | X | X |  |  |  |  |  |

Figure 17: Illustration of Package Mapping Matrix View

# 2.4 Functional Service Area

*Functional Area* (or *Functional Service Area*) defines and captures the system's functional structures (relationships) and behaviors (interactions/collaborations). The center of attention is on the functional behaviors of the application service (user interface service and application business logic service), data service, and technical service, and how these services interact with other system elements.

When collaborating or structuring services, architects need to always reference good practices such as SOLID[28] design principles, and form a thinking framework by asking the following questions:

— What are the *functional responsibilities* assigned to each service?
— How is the service *coupling* (along with the service cohesion and dependency)?
— How is the *granularity* of the service? Why is it justified?
— Does application business logic glue into the generic routines or utility functions (*isolation* of technology or generic logic from business logic)?
— Is service only dependent on services in the same layer or the one below (*layering*), or how is the association with prevailing patterns such as MVC[29] or ECB[30]?
— How will the functional behaviors impact the *non-functional requirement* (NFR)?

By and large, interaction or relationship views have additional usages, such as morphing into an event framework service and the like when needed.

From a domain modeling perspective, the *Functional Area* inbreeds similar thinking logics in a *"composing service"* approach, pivotal for the interplay between business architecture and application system architecture and between modularity and integrality.

Some business folks and techies would argue for a required *Data View* specification, yet in the enterprise solution space, data is cross-cutting in nature. Data service relationships are incrementally built and cross-validated from the data services during the functional modeling process. Consequently, the *Data Service Relationship View* will be reflected from functional, operational, and validation views or purposefully specified in a model view to achieve the same data-driven architectural effect.

---

[28] Single Responsibility, Open Closeness, Liskov Substitution, Interface Segregation, and Dependence Inversion
[29] Model-View-Controller Pattern
[30] Entity-Control-Boundary Pattern, a variation of MVC

# 2.4.1 Service Relationship View

The *Service Relationship View* reflects the structure and modularity of services as well as their dependencies. It's a static view showing the whole relationship of a system or defined domain. As such, there is only one primary relationship view, paired with a couple of expanded views, for each defined service model. Its representation is similar to UML's component relationship view and component structure.

Figure 18 is an illustrative example of the *Service Relationship View*. It's recommended that the *Service Relationship View* be presented by layer or domain following the dependency inversion principle (DIP), as seen in the case study (Figure 48).

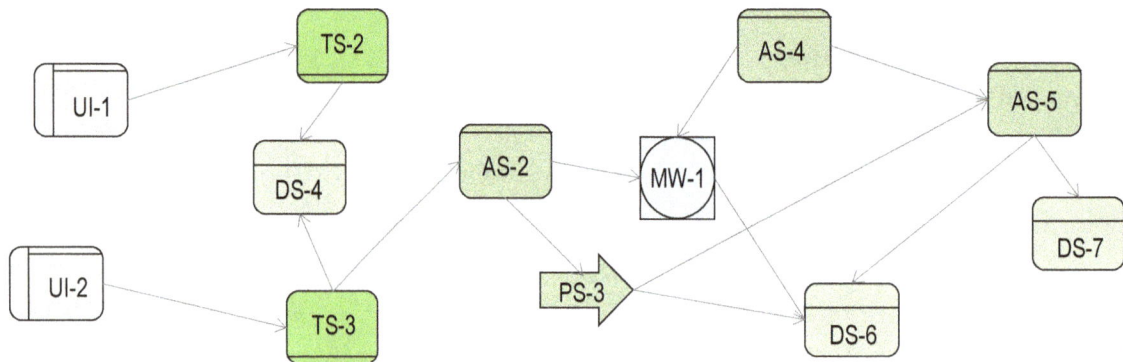

Figure 18: Illustration of Service Relationship View

# 2.4.2 Service Interaction View

The *Service Interaction View* is dynamic, typically reflecting a use-case scenario. The more use-cases, the more interaction views. It's similar to UML's component collaboration view and component sequence view but in a simpler format. The interaction's focal point of services and their behaviors lies in an ideal *sunny-day* situation (see an illustrative view in Figure 19).

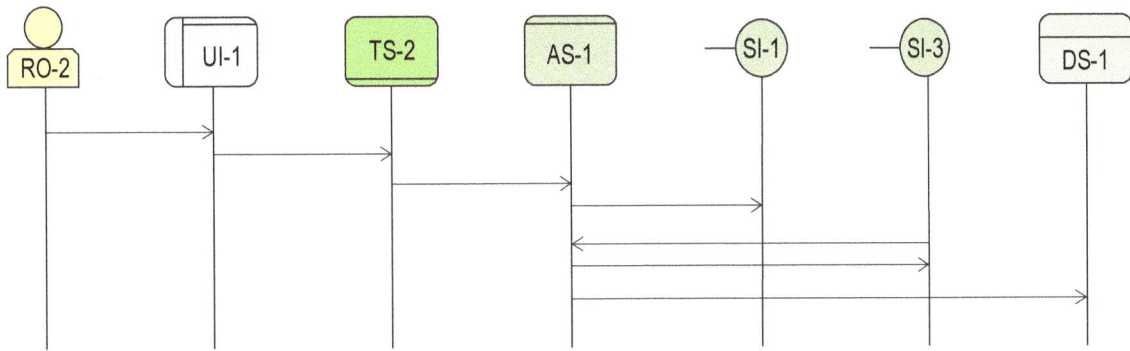

Figure 19: Illustration of Service Interaction View

This view can portray a process service or composite service expressing a long or short flow. The long flow can involve multifaceted human roles, while the short flow is rule-based or straight-through without human interaction, generally done by a technical composite service.

# 2.4.3 Service Component Realization View

In a solution environment, an architect answers for a smooth transition from a high-level service to a service component realization, especially for the architecturally significant components. Ideally, architectural views could be model-driven until implementation in some cases. However, it's infeasible or unnecessary for a strict linkage between architecture and design/development in large, distributed, and complex solutions. IT architecture almost always embraces a certain level of abstraction. In the *Functional Area*, architecture focuses on how service components and interfaces interact with other service components. Selecting data structures or algorithms implemented within the service components is generally not an architectural concern. However, it's recommended to provide guidance, sample specifications, or standardized templates.

Figure 20 shows the *Service Component Realization View*. More details are commonly recorded in the service component property specifications.

| SC Specification | |
|---|---|
| ID | SC-100 |
| Name | getItemList |
| Parameter | String : orderID |
| Return Result | List<Map> - Map includes cost, quantity |
| Notes | Joint Search - use OPSFedSearch |
| Use Case Association | UC-21 Search Order |
| System Interaction | • SY-1 OPS<br>• SY-12 ODW |
| NFR | RQ-NFR-36 Search Processing Time < 5s |

| SC Implementation | |
|---|---|
| Realization | Build |
| Language /Tools | Java/Spring Boot |
| Pattern /Template | See OPS design doc |
| Logic Chart | getItemList flow chart |
| Special Handling | None |

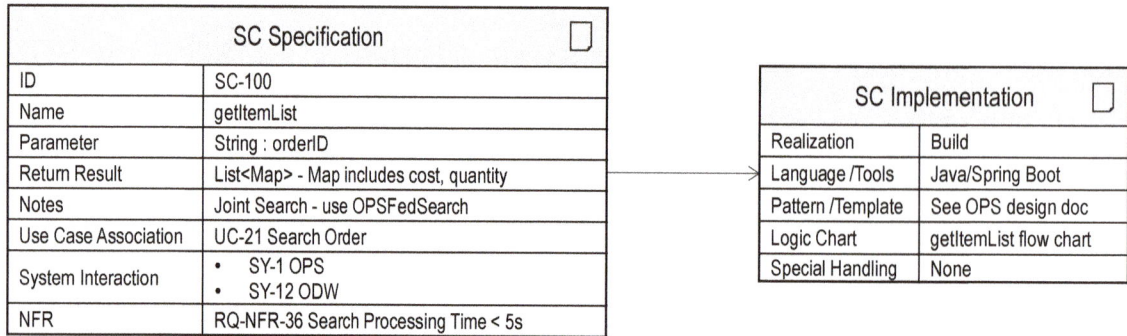

Figure 20: Illustration of Service Component Realization View

This level of detail is sufficient to view the system solution architecture in an unclouded picture. This book does not include any detailed design, componentry, or coding to avoid misleading readers. If architects dive further into the details, they may have gone way off course and crossed the boundary into design space.

Modeling development is an *iterative process*, not just a top-down approach. It can be initiated from a bottom-up approach or somewhere in the middle. A reverse engineering approach would also help architectural transformation by leveraging legacy systems' assets and repositories.

# 2.5 Infrastructural Area

An *Infrastructural Area* (or *Operational Area*) represents how application services are mapped with runtime packages and where the service components are deployed across various locations or zones. Intrinsically, this area reflects how *service level agreements* are fulfilled.

More or less, the *Functional Area* centers on software engineering, while the *Operational Area* focuses on system engineering. Generally, the *Functional Area* drives the *Operational Area*, and operational architecture will inversely impact functional service architecture.

This area relates to system architecture, where systems, middleware, or microservices serve to automate operationalized work. It also fairly relates to technology architecture where IT infrastructure, such as nodes and networks, supports the solution.

In the cloud environment, node provisioning, for example, can be done automatically by PaaS[31] for HA[32] and performance, based on the workload. Even in an automated environment, enterprise solution architects still need to undoubtedly define the IT services and their connections, address cloud security concerns, create capacity planning, and make throughput estimation. They need to further dig into data concerns (such as encryption, archiving and auditing), detect network latency and connection issues in an inherently complex hybrid-cloud setting, and determine the level of SLA support through the *Deployment Views* or operational runtime *Walk-thru Views* in the *Infrastructural Area*.

# 2.5.1 Package Mapping View

The *Deployment Package Mapping View* (or *Package Mapping View* for short) maps each functional service into a runtime package by considering its *unique characteristics* (refer to Table 14). This is critical for the transition from the functional to the infrastructural area. Indeed, how services are packaged is dramatically impactful in the operational runtime environment (see an illustration in Figure 21). In some cases, the *Deployment Package Mapping View* can also be presented in a tabular form when the mapping is straightforward.

Package deployment is a decision-making process by placing various packages based on the metrics view's key considerations, ensuring the system's functional and non-functional requirements are met. Manipulating various placement alternatives leads to a thorough understanding of how NFR matters in packaged containers and middleware server environments, and a likely recombination of functional services adaptable to changing requirements or constraints.

---

[31] Platform as a Service
[32] High Availability

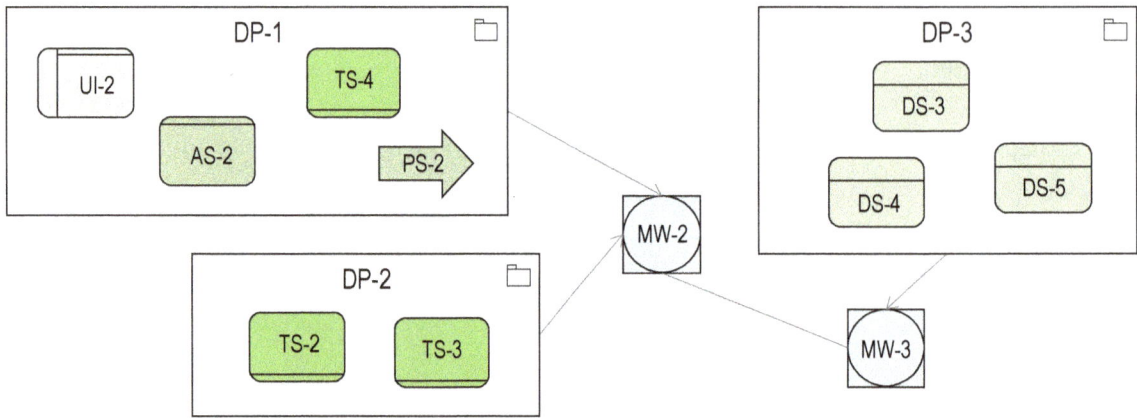

Figure 21: Illustration of Package Mapping View

# 2.5.2 Deployment View

The *Deployment View* represents an operational environment where middleware containing deployment packages is associated with its assigned node (see an illustration in Figure 22), or how deployment packages are placed onto nodes, based on service-level characteristics.

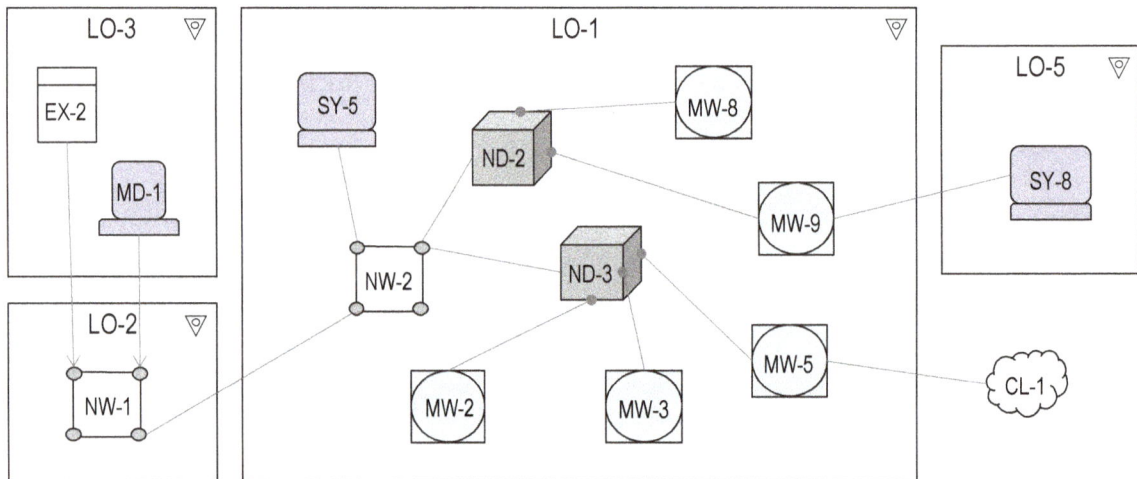

Figure 22: Illustration of Deployment View

The *Deployment View* can be rendered in either the *logical* or *physical* view. The physical view is oftentimes used whereas the logical view is better drafted for reuse. Moreover, the view can be presented in either a structural or dynamic form. The dynamic form is typically an operational walkthrough.

The *Operational Walkthrough View*, simulating coarse-grained failure injections, is a powerful way of testing various *"what-if"* scenarios. For example, what if a connection fails, and what if a deployment package dysfunctions. It's the primary view identifying the root cause of a potential failure and hot spots. It's also the operational view for sizing, reactive-scaling, disruptive changes, single-point failure, caching, disaster recovery, etc. in the key NFR areas of performance, availability, and security. Furthermore, various estimation methods, such as RBD,[33] FTA,[34] and the Parametric Costs Model, can be applied or compared within an experimental walkthrough scenario.

---

[33] Reliability Block Diagram
[34] Fault Tree Analysis

# Chapter 3  A-ESA Elements

*"Weniger, aber besser (less but better)…" — Dieter Rams*

The A-ESA model uses a set of element iconography to describe common concerns surrounding enterprise solution architecture. The role of a chief architect (or lead architect) in the field of enterprise system solution architecture is to address key stakeholder concerns by mapping their requirements to the to-be architecture elements and creating architecture views that take all critical capabilities and relationships into consideration.

By emphasizing service-orientation, the model covers elements of IT services that can be realized by component and/or product. However, it's not from soup to nuts. The granularity of this model does not support *object* concepts (data object, business object, and so on) to avoid the complexity of further drill-down. The model dwells on the external view and depicts what the system has to do for its environment (*black-box effect*), rather than assuming an internal view and depicting how it performs (*white-box effect*). In other words, the architectural elements defined in this book are not meant for detailed architectural design work. As essential as it is, a certain level of abstraction is required during the modeling process.

Table 6 lists model elements, which are classified as basic elements, core elements, and required IT service-based system elements.
— *Basic elements* (28) constitute a full spectrum of solution architecture.
— *Core elements* (20) establish the fundamental elements of solution architecture, from guiding input elements to operational elements.

— *IT system elements* (12) are the key elements for an enterprise solution system to function and operate.

| Category | Element | Abbr | Basic | Core | System |
|---|---|---|---|---|---|
| Enterprise | Capability | CP | x | x | |
| Case Scenario | Role | RO | x | x | |
| | Task | TK | x | x | |
| | Use Case | UC | x | x | |
| Metrics | Principle | PR | x | x | |
| | Requirement | RQ | x | x | |
| | Key Choice | KC | x | x | |
| | Risk | RK | x | x | |
| | Governance | GV | x | x | |
| Function | GUI Service | UI | x | x | x |
| | App Logic Service | AS | x | x | x |
| | Data Service | DS | x | x | x |
| | Tech Service | TS | x | x | x |
| | Service Interface | SI | x | x | x |
| | Service Component | SC | x | | x |
| Infrastructure | Deployment Package | DP | x | x | x |
| | Middleware | MW | x | x | x |
| | System/Device | SY | x | x | x |
| | Node | ND | x | x | x |
| | Network | NW | x | x | x |
| | Location | LO | x | x | x |
| Connection | Association | AN | x | | |
| | Flow | FW | x | | |
| | Composition | CN | | | |
| | Realization | RN | | | |
| General | Grouping/Boundary | GP | x | | |
| | Domain | DM | x | | |
| | Note | NT | x | | |
| | View Frame | VF | x | | |
| | Generic Service | GS | x | | |
| Assistive (Optional) | Cloud Service | CL | | | |
| | Product | PD | | | |
| | Application | AP | | | |
| | Mobile Device | MD | | | |
| | DB Store | DB | | | |
| | Composite – Process | PS | | | |

| Category | Element | Abbr | Basic | Core | System |
|---|---|---|---|---|---|
| | Virtual Service | VS | | | |
| | Virtual Node | VN | | | |
| | Extension/Stereotype | EX | | | |
| Note: — IT functional service elements, the key elements for solution development, require application domain know-how and software engineering effort. | | | | | |

Table 6: List of Elements

Elements can be displayed in four modes: standard mode, icon mode, image mode, or containment mode (Table 7).

| Mode | Text | Icon | Image | Containment |
|---|---|---|---|---|
| Description | This mode is for elements that display relatively more text content | This is a common mode for succinct display | This mode emphasizes physical products or middleware | This mode displays contained elements |
| Example Display | GV-5 Specify distributed transaction framework | MW MDM server | maven | LO Third Party / EX Warehouse / SY Supplier System / SY Bank Agency |

Table 7: Element Display Modes

As shown in Table 8, each core element (while applicable to other views) is associated with a primary view.

| # | Element | Primary View Association |
|---|---|---|
| 1 | Capability (CP) | Capability View (CAP) |
| 2 | Role (RO) | Use Case Model View (UCM) |
| 3 | Task (TK) | Process Management View (PRM) |
| 4 | Use Case (UC) | Use Case Model View (UCM) |
| 5 | GUI Service (UI) | Service Interaction View (SIV) |
| 6 | Application Logic Service (AS) | Service Interaction View (SIV) |
| 7 | Data Service (DS) | Service Relationship View (SRV) |
| 8 | Technical Service (TS) | Service Relationship View (SRV) |
| 9 | Service Interface (SI) | Service Relationship View (SRV) |
| 10 | Deployment Package (DP) | Deployment Mapping View (DPM) |
| 11 | Node (ND) | Deployment View (DEP) |
| 12 | Network (NW) | Deployment View (DEP) |

| # | Element | Primary View Association |
|---|---------|------------------------|
| 13 | Location (LO) | Deployment View (DEP) |
| 14 | Middleware (MW) | Deployment View (DEP) |
| 15 | System/Device (SY) | Architecture Overview View (AOV) |
| 16 | Principle (PR) | Metrics View (MTS) |
| 17 | Requirement (RQ) | Metrics View (MTS) |
| 18 | Key Choice (KC) | Metrics View (MTS) |
| 19 | Risk (RK) | Metrics View (MTS) |
| 20 | Governance (GV) | Metrics View (MTS) |

Table 8: Core Element and its associated Primary View

Figure 23 presents the 20 core elements by group. The four groups of elements lay the foundation for the modeling of the entire enterprise solution architecture.

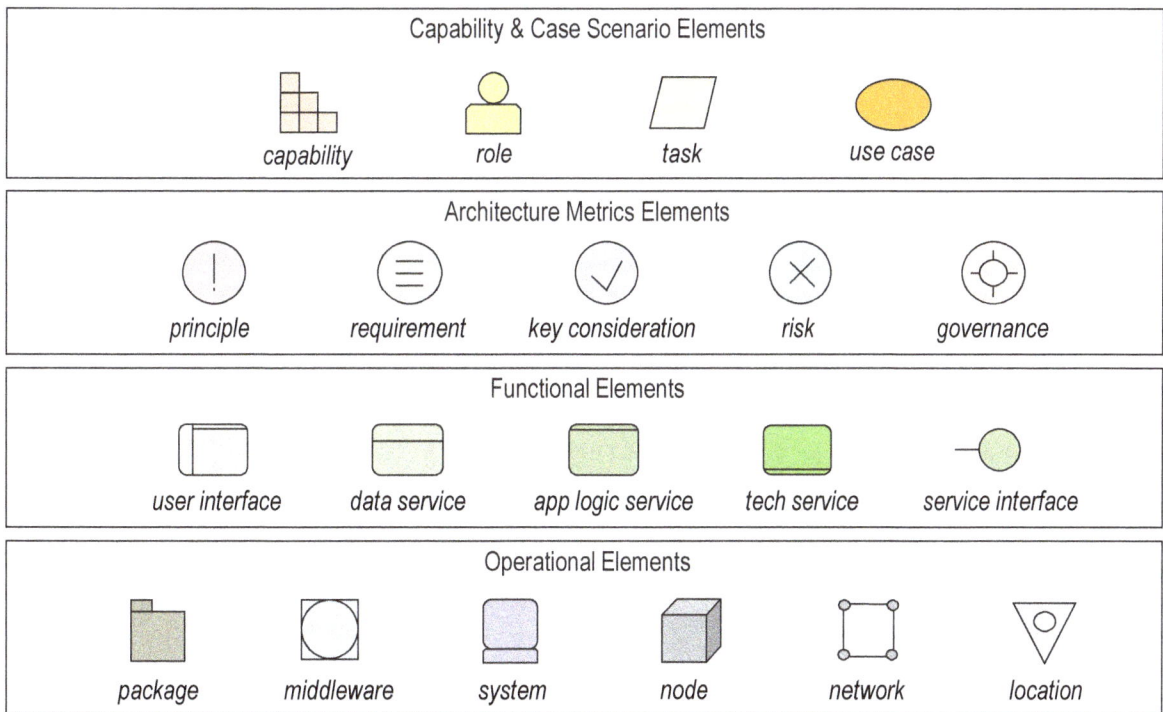

Figure 23: Core Elements by Group

The following sections briefly describe each model element. The simple definition given for each element leverages IT standards as far as possible while fitting to its enterprise solution architectural context.

# 3.1 Enterprise Elements

Enterprise elements are mainly concerned with such enterprise definitions as the user group, business (or technical) domain, principle, and eventually architecture building blocks. Capability is a typical element identified in the *Enterprise Area*.

## 3.1.1 Capability Element

Simple definition:

A *Capability* (CP) represents an EA-level ability that a structural element (such as a functional service) possesses.

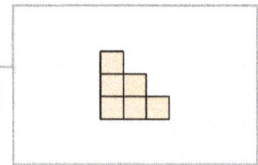

In the agile ESA, attention is given to capabilities related to the IT system solution. *Capability* is thought of as an enterprise building block for the solution architecture. It represents a connection between enterprise architecture and solution architecture, as well as a connection between business and IT. *Capability* can be tagged as being either in a to-be or as-is state.

The lowest level of capability maps to services realized by service components. Service is defined as the value delivery enabled by one or more capabilities. Please note that the capability-associated service offering or API repository content is iterative and enriched throughout the solution architecture and development. At the portfolio level, the structural solution releases (product, system, service, etc.) eventually build up the capabilities of the enterprise.

# 3.2 Case Scenario Elements

At the case scenario stage, the focus is on requirement mapping and not requirement gathering. All of the inputs are obtained either from customer ends or *representations* of customer requirements. For the sake of simplicity, only three required elements (role, use-case, and task) are counted, with the *Generic Service* serving as an optional element.

## 3.2.1 Role Element

Simple definition:

A *Role* (RO) is a responsibility for performing specific behavior, representing a user or user group.

The term *Role* in this work is interchangeable with the term *User Actor*, though they can have a many-to-one relationship. From a service-orientation perspective, the role is more applicable in the architectural context. A *Role Element* is primarily associated with the use-case, the task in a process, and the GUI service in the application functions. A role can loosely stand for a user or user group (part of an actor), an organization, or stakeholder(s).

## 3.2.2 Use Case Element

Simple definition:

A *Use Case* (UC) delineates the interactions between a role and a system to achieve a goal.

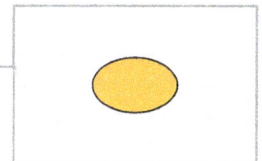

The *Use Case Model View* (containing *Use Case Elements*) provides a sufficiently visual description of what business service is intended from a solution perspective. The formal usage of stereotype expression such as <<extend>> can be ignored for simplicity. A list of actions or event steps can be specified from the use-case properties.

There are two types of use-case elements: *Business Use Case Element* and *System Use Case Element*. Apparently, business use-cases are those that are done manually, and system use-cases are those that are automated by the system.

# 3.2.3 Task Element

Simple definition:

A *Task* (TK) is a piece of work assigned to a role in a process.

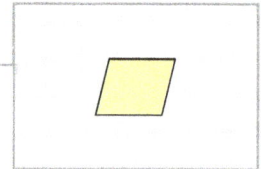

For the sake of simplicity, all activities (or functional points in a process) are referred to as *Task Elements*. Based on the general definition, an activity differs from the task. Some activities are atomic (task or function) while others are not (process and sub-process), as they can be further decomposed. All activities in this book are referred to as tasks carried out within IT services, either as atomic services or composite services. A task can be automatic, semi-automatic, or manual. Automatic and semi-automatic tasks are realized through IT services.

First and foremost, a task has data association. Data item, which is part of the task property, can be specified for data service deliberation later on. Data service results from incorporating task data items into application services. It can also result from other sources such as legacy application and data entity access.

As this book emphasizes the IT services that need to be automated, it's suggested that the term *Task* be used instead of *Business Activity Service*, though a task could be a business activity by nature.

# 3.3 Metrics Elements

Metrics elements facilitate overall architectural thinking and rethinking, and ensure the solution architecture is requirement-abiding and risk-free. They are primarily used in the *Architecture Overview Area* but may originate from an alternative area, as seen in Table 9.

| Metrics Element | Primary Source Area | As Input | As Output |
|---|---|---|---|
| Principle | — Enterprise | Y | |
| Requirement | — Case Scenario | Y | |
| Key Choice | — Architecture Overview | Y | Y |
| Risk | — Architecture Overview | | Y |
| Governance | — Architecture Overview | Y | |
| Note: <br> — The *Key Choice Element* is generally treated as an output element but can also be referred to as an input to the solution(s). <br> — The *Risk* is the potential issue or constraint that needs to be contained. | | | |

Table 9: Source of Metrics Elements

A metrics element is essentially a measurement of architectural viability. It is related to the goals of the user, system, and business. During metrics mapping, these goals need to be balanced.

# 3.3.1 Architecture Principle Element

Simple definition:

An *Architecture Principle* (AP) represents a qualitative statement of intent that must be met by the architecture.

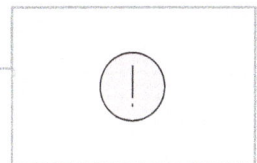

The *Architecture Principle Element* (or *Principle Element* for short) represents all otherwise directional elements, such as goals and drivers, as each architecture principle would be related indirectly to business objectives and key architecture drivers. Principle represents an obligatory intent and partially reflects a business motivation model (BMM)

that has architectural connotations.

The principle (which commonly arises from EA) is enduring, seldom amended and can be set at different levels: guiding principle, or solution (information, technology, and the like) principle. The principles for breaking down microservices, for example, could simply cover bounded contextual boundaries, as well as encapsulation, decentralization, and automation.

Where do the principles come from then? Potential input sources include enterprise missions and plans, CxO's speeches, strategic visions and initiatives, business and technical issues, value propositions, pain points, market factors, industry trends, digital strategies, leading practices, and IT technologies, among others.

The principle plays a key role in the agile enterprise system solution architecture, as seen in Amazon's service interface mandate:

— *"All teams will henceforth expose their data and functionality through service interfaces; anyone who doesn't do this will be fired." —Jeff Bezos, Amazon CEO*

There are a couple of *hints* when applying principles:

— Define as few principles as possible; the maximum number of principles should fit into a poster sheet.
— Make sure the principles are understandable, complete, consistent, robust, and stable.
— Measure principles against architectural considerations.

Architecture principles define the underlying rules and guidelines for using IT resources and assets across the enterprise. They reflect a level of consensus among the enterprise's various elements and form the basis for future IT decisions. In a sense, architecture principles dominantly determine what the enterprise solution architecture will look like.

Table 10 is a principle template defined by the Open Group, and Table 11 shows an example of usage.

| Property | Description |
|---|---|
| Name | Should both represent the essence of the rule as well as be easy to remember. |
| Statement | Should succinctly and unambiguously communicate the fundamental rule. |
| Rationale | Should highlight the business benefits of adhering to the principle, using business terminology. |
| Implication | Should highlight the requirements, both for the business and IT, for carrying out the principle in terms of tasks, costs, etc. |

Table 10: The Open Group's Principle Template

| Property | Description |
|---|---|
| Name | Symmetrical date centers |
| Statement | The primary and secondary data centers should, as far as possible, be mirror images of each other, allowing workloads to migrate between data centers with minimal reconfiguration. |
| Rationale | More agile workload migration between data centers is beneficial, and allows for easier future implementation of high-availability clusters across the data centers. |
| Implication | The link between sites requires an architecture review to harness the full benefit of symmetrical data centers; symmetry needs application migration and re-architecture planning, otherwise infrastructure resources will be idle. |

Table 11: An Example of Architecture Principle

Understanding principles is not a hard row to hoe, but the execution of principles requires systematic enterprise solution modeling and governance.

# 3.3.2 Requirement Element

Simple definition:

A *Requirement* (RQ) represents a succinct statement of needs in a broad sense.

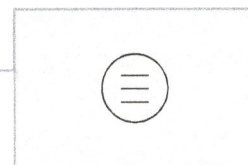

The *Requirement Element* includes business/functional requirements, non-functional requirements (service-level requirements), and rules. Functional requirements are mainly business requirements boiled down to measurable statements. Non-functional requirements include *quality* requirements (including user-end and system-end requirements) and *constraints* (business, legal, technical, etc.). Rules optionally include customized standard, specification, solution-KPI or KAI.[35]

Requirement specifications can be recorded as *Requirement Element* properties, mainly as a functional requirement (FR) or non-functional requirement (NFR):

- FR properties contain business-related functions that an IT system supports and include obvious items such as key business requirement features (functions and processes), roles and responsibilities, business values, and relationships with other business situations.
- NFR properties include user or system-end quality requirements or constraints and specify measurement units, current/target value, best/worst acceptable value, and stress case (peak/burst). It can also include more specific non-functional requirement items such as firewall throughput, network path efficiency, load sharing, and fault tolerance.

*NFR is the very heart and soul of solution architecture.* It is typically a long list in an enterprise solution, ideally containing evidence-based measurement benchmarks. Generally, user-end quality NFRs include performance, availability, security, system management (monitoring, etc.), usability, and accessibility. System-end quality NFRs include portability, interoperability, compatibility, maintainability, modifiability, variability, flexibility, scalability, resilience, data integrity, safety, capacity/evolvability, utilization efficiency, reusability, business continuity, recoverability, stability, and reliability. In fact, a rather fixed structure for a non-functional requirement list can be created, based on SQuaRE[36] (including ISO/IEC 25010, ISO/IEC 25012, and ISO/IEC 25030 standards), Oasis Business QoS[37] Specification, etc. NFRs must be measurable by a series of criteria, such as SLC,[38] service level objectives (SLOs), and the like. Of all the NFRs, those held in the highest regard are performance, availability, security, and systems management – PASS as a mnemonic.

In terms of effective NFR management, experience shows that the Stub and Skeleton approach effectively prevents runtime NFR failures through modeling and simulation. Also, service-oriented architecture, where calls to services can be independently

---

[35] Key Activity Indicator
[36] Systems and software quality requirements and evaluation
[37] Quality of Service
[38] Service-level Characteristics

enabled or disabled, increases system architecture's resilience in a changing NFR environment.

Requirement specifications generally follow the old-fashioned SMART rule: specific, measurable, attainable, realizable, and traceable. They are better expressed in a simple metrics format and prioritized using the MoSCoW[39] method.

In essence, an architect's role in the modeling process is to do *requirement mapping* (between case scenario inputs and solution architecture), not simply requirement gathering, or detailed requirement listing. Not all scenario inputs matter; only architecturally significant requirements need to be considered.

# 3.3.3 Key Choice Element

Simple definition:

A *Key Choice* (KC) is an architecturally significant decision or solution assurance.

The key choice (sometimes referred to as the key consideration) for significant concerns involves assessing various solution options, including architectural decision-making. This key choice is traditionally termed in the geek context as an *Architecture Decision*. An architect's key role is to balance requirements and *constraints*, thus leading to considered decisions, and making optimum use of appropriate frameworks or technologies.

So, the *Key/Architectural Choice* is the central part of architectural thinking, from the unreasoned to the reasoned. While routine choices can be taken for granted or automated, effort should be spent on choices that are costly or hard to reverse. The following are advocated consideration spaces for key decisional choices:

— How the enterprise capabilities are strategically aligned and how activities/tasks are allocated to achieve ideal value streams?

---

[39] Must, Should, Could, or Would

— What architectural style (reference architecture, patterns alike) is chosen to fit each enterprise solution's needs?
— How significant NFRs will be met, through a tradeoff analysis, middleware choice, or modeling?
— How well the solution architecture is holistically validated?

These are situations when the *Key Choice Element* is all the more needed:
— During the initial solution architecture stage or retrospective governance process
— When facing tough decisional choices or touching on cross-cutting areas
— When adopting a new architectural approach or IT technology (reasoning about what lies beyond existing capabilities, potential impact on marketing needs/business benefits, and ROI)

Justification of a key choice develops from a comparison of pros and cons, with a set of pre-defined criteria such as popularity, priority, user impact, and learning curve. Table 12 is a template of the *Key Choice Element* conforming to the architecture decision record (ADR) specifications. Table 13 shows an example of usage.

| Property | Description |
|---|---|
| Statement | A statement of the situation where the consideration is significant, and normally requires a choice to be made. |
| Alternatives | A list of options to choose from. If there are no alternatives, that means an obvious choice of less concern. |
| Decision | A chosen architectural decision |
| Justification | Simple reason why the choice or decision is made |
| Stakeholder | Associated parties in the consideration |
| Criteria (optional) | A list of enterprise solution criteria, potentially with a detailed analysis, for justification |
| Explanation | A description of related concern, impact, likelihood, implication, dependency, rationale, consequence, motivation, assumption, status, etc. |

Table 12: Template of Key Choice

| Property | Description |
|---|---|
| Statement | How do the services talk to each other? |
| Alternatives | 1.   Rest API – JSON over HTTP<br>2.   gRPC – Google's invocation framework |
| Decision | Choice of gRPC |

| Property | Description |
|---|---|
| Justification | 1. Efficient binary encoding, faster than JSON/HPPT<br>2. Clear interface specification, easier to understand than SWAGGER/Open API,<br>3. Streaming support |
| Stakeholder | 1. Architect<br>2. Designer<br>3. Programmer |

Table 13: Example of Key Choice Specification

Solution expertise suggests that many solution issues do not, in fact, come from design or implementation but from architectural considerations. For example, when applying data sharding, architectural trade-offs should be balanced for such discrete alternatives: "dividing up the database and/or table" and "deciding which unique id to use". Each choice has pros and cons, and there is no best choice, only the best effort based on the CAP[40] theorem. And the trade-off between agility and quality is often the problem architects face. The *Key Choice Element* records the key decision-making process and guides the design and implementation work.

A key choice or consideration often takes account of multiple factors coupled with situational awareness and related directions or requirements. For example, when considering internet performance simultaneously with internet access bandwidth and response-time requirements, how can we ensure both low bandwidth and high bandwidth customers have an acceptable user experience?

Vitally, the key choice needs to adhere to some basic solution principles: fitness, simplicity, and evolvability. When following guidelines (including policies and principles), architects need to verify assumptions and provide feedback, if any, to the governing body for potential ameliorations. Decisions can be deferred if sufficient information is not yet available.

Architectural tradeoff analysis, part of decisional architecture, is an ongoing process and should be kept timely as history record for ready reference.

---

[40] Consistency, Availability, and Partition Tolerance

# 3.3.4 Risk Element

Simple definition:

A *Risk* (RK) *Element* represents a potential issue, something that hasn't happened, that needs to be handled.

The *Risk Element* (or *Issue Element*) logs non-trivial risks and issues that need to be handled. It takes general consideration of assumption, dependency, issue resolution, status, likelihood, impact, effort, owner, deadline, priority, recommendation, etc. It can be recorded in the *Risk Element* properties. The risk analysis helps spot tacky solution pieces (high complexity, high effort, and low impact) for failing-fast.

Risk is largely bound to project management (cost/budget, time/schedule, and scope). Yet the risk-related focus of this book is principally on architectural issues (agility, quality, constraint, etc.).

# 3.3.5 Governance Element

Simple definition:

A *Governance* (GV) embodies IT architecture standards, compliance, and assessment criteria.

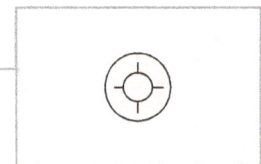

The *Governance Element* is primarily used in the architecture assessment for model enhancement in conformance to normative standards.

This element is about the understanding that in an agile enterprise solution architecture, *control* needs to be in place. Its properties include RACI[41] responsibilities and rating criteria.

---

[41] R – Review, A – Approve, C – Consult, I – Information Only

# 3.4 Functional Elements

The *Functional Area* builds up and correlates IT functional services that are the central part of modeling. Based on the extensive subject matter expertise, the model divides IT functional services into four categories: GUI service, application logic service, data service, and technical service. Each of them has a unique set of quality characteristics that are closely related to runtime behaviors. Additionally, this division obviously enforces a service *layering* to lay a solid foundation of service structure to ensure *service granularity*, *loose-coupling*, and *isolation*. Consequently, this allows for rational and practical mappings between services and packages in the *Infrastructural Area*. Moreover, this division of service facilitates efficiency and coordination of development and maintenance among the GUI team, data team, application development team, and technology team. The rationale for this division is exhibited in Table 14.

| Service Type | Service Quality Characteristics |
|---|---|
| GUI | Type of user/actors, access frequency, concurrency, active time, access mechanism, etc. |
| Application Business Logic | Actor touch point, cohesion, logic complexity, composition, technical isolation, invocation mechanism, etc. |
| Data | Data type, volatility, currency, record size, record numbers, usage intensity, etc. |
| Technical | Concurrent user/actors, transaction type, operating time, bandwidth condition, etc. |

Table 14: Characteristics of IT Services

The *Functional Area* also includes *Service Interface* and *Service Component* elements. These two elements are natural parts of IT services, as the service is a logical containment of one or more service components and reified by service component(s). To an enterprise solution architect, the final deliverable should include a set of well-designed service interfaces. As the saying goes in the IT circle, *all is well when the interfaces are well*.

As mentioned earlier, to foster flexibility and extensibility, the IT service can also be a *Generic Service* type used for initial service specification, business service, a placeholder service, microservice or application service considerations. Please note that the term

*Application Service* here loosely implies GUI, application logic, or data service.

A service that won't finally become a physical IT service is treated as a *Virtual Service* where it normally has no clear interface (say, a script or a template) or is just a service event coordination, interaction, collaboration, or the like.

The agile ESA model emphasizes the black box effect, defining more coarse-grained services and its interfaces and interactions but *not* the details inside a service. In comparison with the component-based architecture, the model is of much higher granularity. As a rule of thumb, the *granularity* of a service depends on the service type and service domain. The purposeful ESA model elements help define granular service levels. For instance, an *Application Logic Service* usually follows the granular chain: generic service – process or composite service (optional) – atomic service – service component, coupled with consideration of capability, domain, and other related elements such as cloud services. Note that the relationships among the functional services of a complex enterprise solution give rise to a whole that can hardly be understood by one level of granularity or insignificant constituents.

For domain service or microservice architectural design, miscellaneous functionality (application logic, data, and technical) may be put together. The same applies to the application service. Depending on the service's nature, it may fall into a *Generic Service* category, a specific functional service category, or an application category.

Notably, the functional services fall squarely in the overlap between business and technology, enabling both business and IT folks to carry meaningful conversations on the solution architecture.

Some might argue that the categorization of functional services could be simplified into application and technical services. If that's the case, then how can they be clearly mapped with other functional services with unique runtime characteristics? For instance, how would the data service be dealt with in the development and deployment environment? How would the graphical user interaction service be tailor-made to meet its non-functional requirements while adhering to the principle of isolating navigation and usability from its application business logic?

# 3.4.1 GUI Service Element

Simple definition:

A *GUI Service* (UI) is an interactive service with a visual presentation.

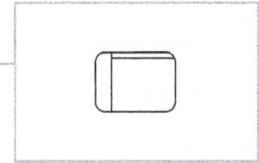

GUI services are normally done by a specialized team or division, following common specifications or standards, including multi-experience development specifications.

*GUI Service Element* contains an *implicit interface* and may have an *explicit interface* or API to expose visual service for remote presentation in a service-orientation environment.

# 3.4.2 Application Logic Service Element

Simple definition:

An *Application Logic Service* (AS) represents explicitly defined non-GUI application behaviors and control logic.

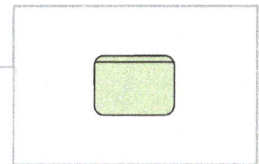

As its name suggests, application business logic service or application logic service (or app logic service for short) is application-specific, containing logic to fulfill business requirements. An *Application Logic Service Element* exposes the functionality of service components to their environment. This functionality is accessed through one or more service component interfaces.

*App Logic Service Element* can handle functions or take the form of a business logic process service (composite service), which is a sequence of business logic behaviors that achieves a specific outcome. It can involve non-GUI interaction service or collaboration service.

Broadly speaking, application logic services are often referred to as application services, application business services, or business services, among other names. Business services and application services are sometimes interpreted as two sides of the same coin. Traditionally, application services contain a GUI service, application business service, or data service. An application service differs from an application, which is a piece of software runtime from user views. To avoid confusion, this book refrains from using the terms "application service" and "business service" in the architecture work product when "application logic service" is the intended meaning.

Applications invariably require state management, but it's typically better when individual services are *stateless*. As part of the *App Logic Service Element*, the composite or process choreographer (or service consumer) assumes state management responsibilities. Common state considerations include functional state, transaction state, and security state. Certain state-intensive activities can be managed by dedicated finite state machine (FSM) logic services.

# 3.4.3 Data Service Element

Simple definition:

A *Data Service* (DS) is a self-contained piece of information that has a clear meaning to the business.

According to the Data Service Framework, data service is a general term of data provision, data fabric, data platform, and data analytics that covers all levels of data services from data collection, data processing, data reuse, and data analysis to provide business insights.

Examples of data services are customer service, order management service, insurance claim service, federated data service, and database service. From the perspective of the data demand side, modern data service suppliers are more than just traditional data collectors because they provide data services that support the business process and management decision-making of data demanders, resulting in Data as a Service (DaaS) or Big Data as a Service (BDaaS).

A *Data Service Element* represents well-structured data ready for use, taking account of its performance, reusability, and consistency. Data service often involves technical service or business logic services (data domain-specific), but it represents a data offer, not a functional interface. A data service can also take the form of a composite service whereby a sequence of data logic behaviors is processed. The granularity of a data service is determined by the business context. In this model, the domain or group element largely serves to assemble related data services. Data service properties include security requirements, compliance, and real-time (or batch) processing. Even though data make up an essential part of the runtime, the enterprise solution architecture contains only those data services that map the key requirements for avoiding information overloading.

The *Data Service Relationship View* can be depicted and modified not only from an interaction or relationship view but also from an automatic *Relationship Validation View*. In the model, data's interrelationships with other elements are more accentuated than in a stand-alone data relationship analysis, which is part of the data entity relationship analysis. It's worth mentioning that the commonly known big data service is not merely a data service per se, as it usually requires an *end-to-end process*.

Regarding the *Flow Message* associated with the data service, the model only needs to capture a high-level description of the service messages, including the topic, input message, and output message. Later design activities will create a detailed message specification.

In short, data services lie between the invoking application or interface and the data object or data entity that accesses the data table, database, or data source. An elaboration on data services is largely similar to the entity relationship (ER) model. For the data service property specifications outlined in this book, the data item is conceivably equivalent to the ER's entity. While data services can be analyzed in many subject areas from many viewpoints, entities are more likely to be relevant to only one subject area, as the data model's focus is usually specific to one viewpoint.

# 3.4.4 Technical Service Element

Simple definition:

A *Technical Service* (TS) represents a behavior, unrelated to the application-specific logic context.

A *Technical Service* is more meaningful from the viewpoint of the runtime environment. It may partly play a role in the middleware functionalities. While the middleware is a piece of ready-made software or part of platform service, the technical service is usually subject to homegrown implementation. The technical service offered by the cloud service is virtually a cloud-based or remote middleware service.

Strictly speaking, the *Technical Service Element* (or *Tech Service Element* for short) has two sides of a coin: functional and operational. In a service-orientation architecture, technical service is more functional. Meanwhile its operational nature is embodied in its belonging package and its deployed node after that.

Beware of the difference between technical service and application logic service. The former is more generic, mostly applicable to multifarious projects for general use and wide reuse. In contrast, the latter is more application-specific. Additionally, do not mix up technical service with technology service which includes servers or network products at an infrastructural level.

# 3.4.5 Service Interface Element

Simple definition:

A *Service Interface* (SI) represents a point of access where services are made available to a user, service or service component.

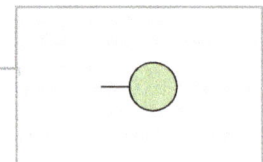

In short, interface refers to *Service Component Interface* or *Service Interface*, given that the component interface is not the primary concern of this model. In other words, the service interface exposes service(s) realized from the service component. Service interface can also be exposed to system components, a server component, node components, and the like when treated as IT services.

The exposed service interface, explicitly with well-defined service interface contracts, is referred to as service API. A good service API provides *coarse-grained* interface contracts and shields the internal complexity of service components. Be cautious, as it's challenging in practice to design APIs not prone to a leaky abstraction situation where an API consumer has to understand unnecessary implementation details. For a monolithic application transformation, the exposed APIs are more likely prone to *abstraction leaks*.

For all implementable service interfaces, they have offering services and consuming services (if any) available to participants via ports. A *Service Interface Element* is virtually *an aggregation of service component interface(s)*. Therefore, underneath the service component interface specification comprises the requester parameter, provider parameter, exposure parameter, and so on. Additionally, it can contain message flow information.

Here are the general rules for identifying service component interfaces:
— From the use-cases, for example:
 — updateAccount() would be a service component interface operation
— From the automated tasks in a long-flow process, for example:
 — the task of recording payment details through a system interface
— From the business data entities or ERD, steps:
 1. identify the core business entities, such as order, or account
 2. create interfaces to handle core business entities, such as IOrderSVC interface, and IAccountSVC interface
— From the existing system application interfaces
— From the non-functional requirement

For service interface specifications, it's recommended to identify service component interfaces of no small consequence. Apply the "80/20" rule, which says 20% of the requirements account for 80% of the user activities.

The *Service Component Interface*, employing IT service offering, differs from the traditional API, oftentimes via a programming interface library using a one-API per-object interface pattern in the object-oriented world. *"A modern API represents a package of capabilities that are attractive to an audience independent of any specific piece of software running in the back end."* Indeed, one of the main objectives of the IT service-based architecture is to separate the service interface (represented by the contract and associated metadata) from the underlying service implementation. In other words, interface implementation is confined within the abstracted IT service boundaries.

The following are some frequently discussed topics about the interface or API:

— *Primary service interfaces and their usage*: Generic service interfaces are abstraction-based, designed for architectural considerations. REST interfaces are resource-based, and suitable for mobile developers. SOAP interfaces are method-based, and good for system integration. MQTT interfaces are event-based, preferred for communicating with IoT- or CQRS-based systems.

— *Product nature of APIs*: APIs, as business products, should be an integral part of business strategy, such as providing a differentiating omnichannel customer experience. APIs can be monetary or based on a nonmonetary value. Based on registered media with a common framework, hypermedia APIs ensure that APIs align with its providers' design goals.

— *APIs vs. services*: Technically, an API is also a service. Services are generally designed with architectural concerns and stability in mind. However, APIs are always designed to cater to the changing needs of the intended consumer as a uniform consumption model in an ecosystem environment. Therefore, APIs and services are not opposing forces, and they are complementary rather than contradictory.

— *Interface vs. contract-based approach*: An interface-based approach is about HOW, while a contract-based approach is about WHAT. For simplicity, the term *service contract* – usually a derivative of the service description – is not applied here.

# 3.4.6 Service Component Element

Simple definition:

A *Service Component* (SC) represents implementing service responsibility or functionality.

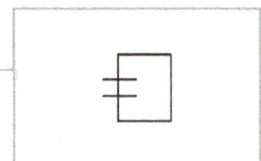

A *Service Component Element* is a self-contained modular unit, technology-specific and replaceable. Service encapsulates its contents, its behavior, or data. Its functionality is only accessible through a set of service-component interfaces.

The granularity of the service component varies. It can be a system-level component or a simple calculation component, conditioned by its usage, functional responsibilities, and distribution.

# 3.5 Infrastructural Elements

An *Infrastructural Area* basically contains elements independent of specific applications. Deployment package, an infrastructural element, plays a role in transforming functional services to the operational environment.

Node, network, and storage (a kind of system) elements fall into a solution infrastructure, and can be part of IaaS[42] in the cloud environment.

## 3.5.1 Package Element

Simple definition:

*A Deployment Package* (PK) contains various functional services based on their unique service-level characteristics.

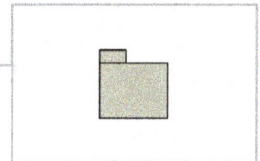

Each deployment package (or package for short) is wrapped up with a group of services with similar SLA. A package represents all the runtime archive files (static or dynamic), executable binary files, or interpreted script files in the physical form of .war, .ear, .exe, .dll files, etc. The package serves as a medium between functional services and their hosting nodes. The package placement decision is based on NFRs or

---

[42] Infrastructure as a Service

balanced between NFRs and node specifications.

The deployment package is similar to the *Deployment Unit* (DU), used in conceptual solution design to represent any facet of an application component at run time or deployment time. As the DU concept is commonly regarded as a bit involved and academic, deployment package is more practical. The deployment package can also be simply referred to as the *Application Package*. Unlike an application, which is a software runtime from user views, an application package is from developer and system deployment perspectives. Noticeably, the application and deployment packages do not need to be 1:1 mapping.

However, in a microservice architecture, a *Package Element* can contain business logic service, data service, and technical service altogether for the sake of quick development, self-containment deployment, and/or distributed operational environment. For microservice deployment, it involves a collection of patterns following a set of key principles (such as antifragility and immutability). Different types of services would be lumped together in the same package.

# 3.5.2 Middleware Element

Simple definition:

A *Middleware* (MW) represents system software that provides services to software applications.

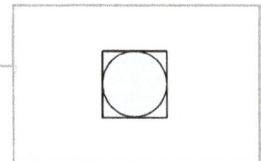

The *Middleware Element* refers to COTS,[43] software glue, ready-made technical service, or technology enabler. Middleware can provide both functional and infrastructural services. Examples of middleware include enterprise development tools, implementation framework, integration software, edge computing, database software, security software, and potentially software-defined network environment. When designed friendlier to the business users, middleware is called *Upper Middleware*,

---

[43] Commercial Off-The-Shelf

offering functional services for stress-free application wirings.

In the ESA, an *Operating System* (OS) is not strictly part of the middleware definition, given that it's more closely attached to a particular hardware node and specified from its property attribute. A typical layer of middleware design can contain interfaces to operating systems. For special NFR considerations, the OS can be treated as a system/device middleware or virtual node.

Middleware, or cloud middleware, is generally categorized by certain criteria; for example, helper services middleware covering security, observability, tracing and debugging, operations, anomaly detection, and application lifecycle management. Figure 24 illustrates middleware categorization using exemplar color shades and icons in a blockchain architecture overview.

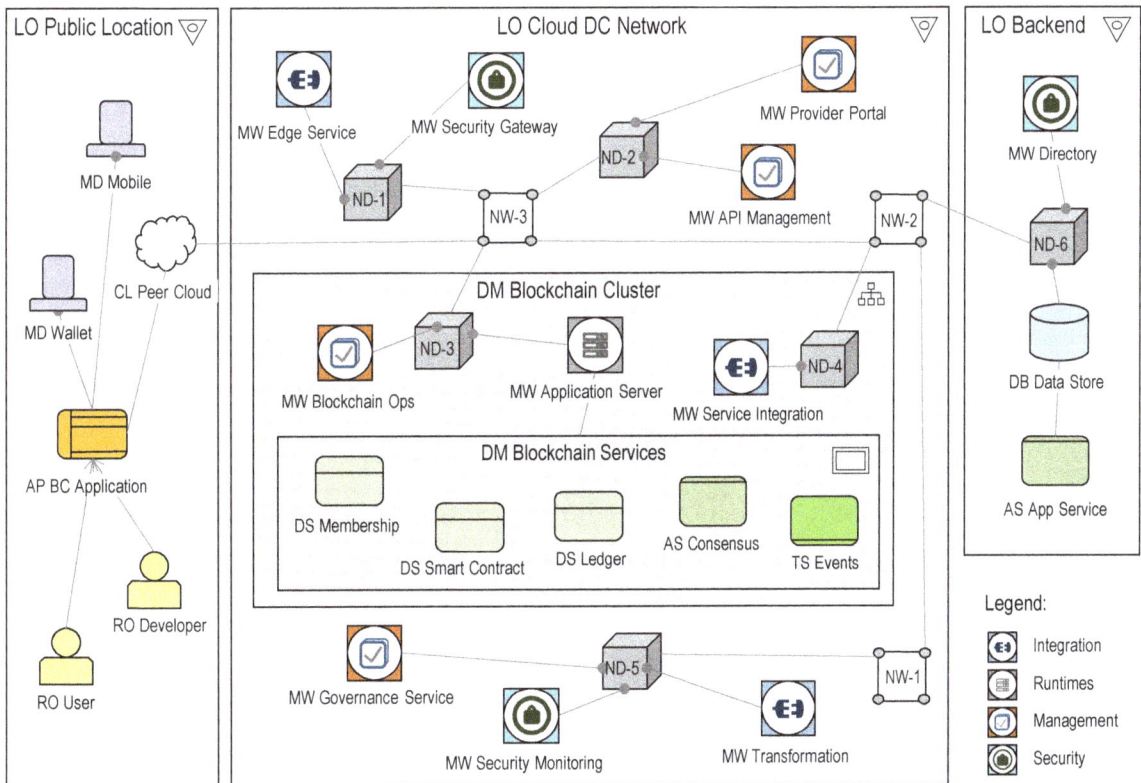

Figure 24: Illustration of Middleware Categorization

In the era of cloud services, tens of thousands of middleware functionalities will be provided from cloud platforms. These middle services are implemented to run across multiple regions. They are robust, rugged, and scalable. In the future, some mega-cloud providers would take control of IT platforms in the world; even then, middleware functionality, or cloud middleware service, is still relevant in the enterprise solution architecture. In FaaS [44] or serverless enabled cloud, platform middleware provides services to the software applications. Similarly, PaaS is formed by the cloud-based middleware.

# 3.5.3 System Element

Simple definition:

An *IT System* (SY) is a collection of hardware and software pieces and a set of relationships for specific business functions.

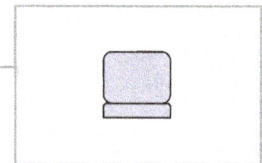

A system (or device) exists to fulfill one or more missions within its environment. Examples of the *System Element* include email systems (e.g., Microsoft Exchange server plus outlook clients), ERP, CRM, MIS, [45] CMDB, [46] supplier systems, and storage systems. The system can be categorized by its key service-level characteristics. In the extreme, there are three very high-level categories of enterprise systems: *system of engagement*, *system of record*, and *system of integration*.

The system, or subsystem, is a loose terminology with distinguished interpretations. Either an enterprise application, mobile device, or hardware device could be named a system. A system does not have an interface alone, and that is the distinction from an *Application Component*, which is a software piece or a collection of services, parts, or objects. It's also a collection of organized pieces different from architecture that is the art and science of crafting solutions.

---

[44] Function as a Service
[45] Management Information System
[46] Configuration Management Database

# 3.5.4 Node Element

Simple definition:

A *Node* (ND) generally represents a hosting resource that interacts with other resources.

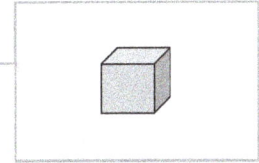

The *Node Element* epitomizes a hardware piece with CPU chips or firmware commonly encompassing operating systems. Examples of a node include server machines, computers, or hardware platforms.

For the simplest definition, a *Virtual Node* is a specialization of a repository that hosts guest software applications. A container is a typical virtual node that runs on a physical node. In a cloud environment, architecture is more about virtual services, not server machines.

# 3.5.5 Network Element

Simple definition:

A *Network* (NW) denotes a set of structures, products, and services that enable system node connections for data transmission.

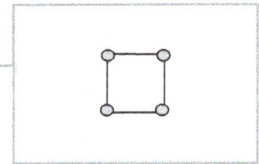

In physical form, the *Network Element* generally refers to hardware pieces of network or software-defined pieces (tightly attached to hardware) that enable a system node's connection. Network-related software generally falls into the middleware element.

Examples of a *Network Element* include firewall, router, switches, hardware gateway, and hardware load balancer.

Note that the agile ESA only provides a network architecture blueprint, so it's not suggested to delve into design details of network integration, security and management.

## 3.5.6 Location Element

Simple definition:

*A Location* (LO) is a place where structural elements are positioned or communicated.

The *Location Element* encompasses geographic or architecturally defined places.

# 3.6 Connection Elements

A connection element represents the relationship between a source element and a target element. The model uses a minimal number of relationships for the simplicity of learning and use. Only four types of relationships are defined, but they have implied connection relationships (Table 15).

| Relationship Type | Implied Relationship |
|---|---|
| Association | — Generic relationship |
| Flow | — Access (control access, protocol, data transmission, etc.)<br>— Triggering (event, etc.)<br>— Serving (service-orientation)<br>— Influence<br>— Dependency (*restricted use*) |
| Composition | — Aggregation<br>— Generalization (*restricted use*) |
| Realization | — Assignment<br>— Specialization |
| Note:<br>— As an embodiment of service-orientation, the *serving relationship* can be expressed using flow connection with the keyword <<serve>>. Generally, an explicit serving relationship is only shown via a relationship connecting an interface at one end. However, it's recommended that an implicit serving relationship be applied, via any of the four connection relationships.<br>— A non-relationship element can connect to a relationship element right in the middle to serve the relationship element. This kind of non-relationship element shape can be flexible (see Figure 66).<br>— Dependency connection type is not emphasized in the model for loosely dependent service orientation. ||

Table 15: Definition of Connection Elements

Traditionally, architectural modeling employs more complex connection relationships. For example, realization and composition are part of the structural relationship, and flow is part of the dynamic relationship. The connection element intentionally disregards strict definitions and blurs the differences between some commonly known architectural element relationships for simplicity. For example, *aggregation* and *composition* are treated the same in the agile ESA approach. However, strictly speaking, they are dissimilar. The former implies a relationship where a child can exist independently of the parent, whereas the latter implies a relationship where the child can't exist independently.

# 3.6.1 Association Relationship Element

Simple definition:

An *Association* represents a generic or an unspecified relationship.

The *Association Element* is the most generic relationship element that is connectible to any non-relationship element.

# 3.6.2 Flow Relationship Element

Simple definition:

A *Flow* represents the movement from one element to another.

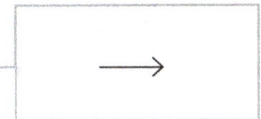

The *Flow Element* connotes any movement relationships including access (control access, protocol, data transmission, etc.), triggering (event, etc.), serving (service-orientation), influence, and dependency.

## 3.6.3 Composition Relationship Element

Simple definition:

*A Composition consists of one or more other elements.*

The *Composition Element* reflects a containing relationship, including aggregation and generalization.

## 3.6.4 Realization Relationship Element

Simple definition:

*A Realization moves from an abstract element to a concrete one.*

The *Realization Element* is a representation of a partnering or materializing relationship, including assignment and specialization.

# 3.7 General Elements

The general elements help architectural modeling for outlining and scoping, and constitute a minimal set of elements for an agile solution architecture.

## 3.7.1 Generic Service Element

Simple definition:

*A Generic Service (GS) covers well-defined business activities in a specific application context.*

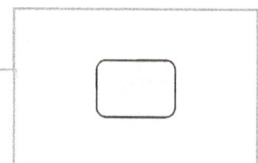

A generic service, or aggregate service, is a loosely defined service from an IT architecture perspective. It can imply a transition between business service and IT service (solution service), business service, or business *function*. In a sense, microservice can be treated as generic service (further down to functional services) unless it targets a specific service, such as technical service for IT automation.

A *Generic Service Element* serves as a liaison between business and IT and can thus be loosely treated as *business service*. By definition, business service is a repeatable and measurable outcome from a business component, a collection of similar activities that share a unique business purpose, such as order-processing management.

Remarkably, business service is likely one of the most debated terms. Some IT practitioners use the term to describe processes or activities driven by the lines of business or functions used by end-customers of a company or its employees. Others use the term as a means of distinguishing between applications and technology infrastructure. Many people are confused about business service and application service. Actually, a key criterion in distinguishing the two is whether the service system is primarily defined by its dependence on computing and information management resources. Simply put, any service that is not part of the IT services could be referred to as a business service. A simple distinction can be made from the following definition:
— Human to Human service – business service
— IT to Human service – IT service
— IT to IT service – IT service

For simplified overall architecture, it's not recommended to use the term *business service* and its associated business-component concepts. Quite a few IT thought leaders believe that the term should be eliminated from the IT vocabulary. This avoids the common questioning of the nuance disparity between the business service at an architectural business level and at an architectural application level. However, in the requirement area, the term business service can still be used for convenient discussions with customers.

Rather than the business architecture, this model centers around the system architecture, so the *Generic Service Element* means less strictly-defined business service in a special solution context. The *business goal, objective, or KPI (a must for BPM[47])* are not a very caring subject. Business objectives will be partially reflected in the architectural principles and business requirements, recorded in the related view/element properties.

# 3.7.2 Note Element

Simple definition:

A *Note* (NT) represents the comment or interpretation of the architecture.

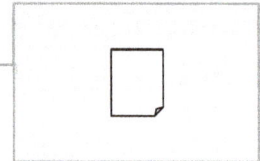

The *Note Element* only shows the critical information that needs to be highlighted in a view or the information not suitable for property recording. The note element also denotes meaning, and value. It can be rendered in a rich text format, making it a more flexible presentation element.

# 3.7.3 View Frame Element

Simple definition:

A *View Frame* (VF) serves to help scale an architectural blueprint design.

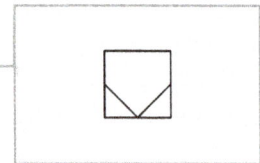

The *View Frame Element* is primarily for easy reference, partial view, or nesting view. It generally functions as a drill-down mapping to its corresponding view element. As a snapshot element, it can serve as a *plateau*[48] element. The plateau can also reflect solution release stages where solution sprints[49] are aggregated.

More importantly, the model view (a purposed thinking block) can form a bigger

---

[47] Business Process Management
[48] A plateau represents a relatively stable state of the architecture that exists during a limited period of time.
[49] Solution Increments

enterprise solution picture via associated view frame elements. By the same token, boiling a complicated model view down to the fundamental view frames helps *reason from first principles* (a systematic approach to generate original solutions) to simplify significant solution issues at different layers of *architectural abstraction*.

# 3.7.4 Group Element

Simple definition:

A *Group* (GP) represents a generic composition or aggregation of elements.

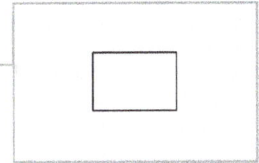

A *Group Element* (or *Grouping Element*) is an element for generic grouping. Table 16 shows the typical *Group Element* usage.

| Usage Type | Explanation |
|---|---|
| Generic | Grouping without restrictions under the same scope |
| Layering | Grouping elements by block, or logically lying elements between two other strata |
| Note: — A conceptual grouping does not enforce element relationships, and can be represented by dash lines or dotted lines. — Another usage of grouping is for modeling domains, as seen in the TOGAF framework's definition of Information Domains (grouping by a set of criteria such as security classification, ownership, location, etc.). | |

Table 16: Group Element Usage

# 3.7.5 Domain Element

Simple definition:

A *Domain* (DM) is a concept of the boundary in which multiple elements are controlled under the same scope.

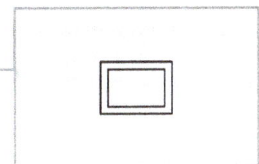

The *Domain Element* is used primarily for large system architecture and characterized by functional scope, operational scale, and change frequency. By partitioning functional or infrastructural building blocks by domain, it's easier to determine physical boundaries for the reasons of functional partition, data processing, transactional integrity, reuse, scalability, responsive workload, and virtual environment. Table 17 shows the common domain usage in enterprise solution architecture. It is based on the results of many projects experiences and for reference use only.

| Usage | Type | Explanation |
|---|---|---|
| Generic | Domain | It indicates a generic domain. |
| | Scope | It represents the breath, depth or reach of a subject. For example, a project scope with a set of project goals, timelines, tasks, deliverables, etc. |
| | Context | It's a boundary (business, system, or application). For example, a system context that separates internal components of a system from external entities. |
| Operational Processing | Transaction | It's a sequence of one or more data operations that are treated as a unit to ensure ACID.[50] |
| | Clustering | It enables a single point of management across visibility nodes. |
| Partition | Environment | It's a complete structure within which a user, computer, or program operates. Example: testing, QA, production, etc. |
| | Platform | It's an underlying computer system (hardware and software) on which application programs can run. Example: system/390. |
| | Tier | It's a physical group of system elements within an environment such as a located server fleet. |
| | Region | It's a cordoned-off geographical location with zone(s), depending on the context. |
| | Zone | It's an aggregation of several model elements for which a common set of values for a particular kind of requirement (commonly operational) is defined. For example, network security zones, applied to an organization, can contain internet (uncontrolled zone), labeling as Red. By internet definition, a zone is physical while a domain is a logical DNS name space. |

Note:
— The term *Domain* varies by definition. For less restrictions, use *Group Element* instead.
— The popular term "middle platform" or "mid-platform" is not meant merely as a technical platform domain. It's a packaged business capability platform domain with shared service offerings.

Table 17: Common Domain Usage

---

[50] Atomicity, Consistency, Isolation, and Durability

It's worth mentioning that Domain-Driven Design (DDD) portrays a nice way of forming a business or functional domain in theory. However, in practice, the determination of the domain or granularity of services is an art, requiring business acumen and architectural technique. None of the well-known methods, be it SOMA,[51] DDD, DDM[52] or Clean Architecture, can replace a domain expert or subject matter expert (SME) in a specific area of expertise. More or less, a practical and well-designed *service* domain can be made possible through the modeling context via the four functional services and group/domain elements, with the help of a context map and/or bounded context knowledge. Nevertheless, it is not advised to touch software engineering design terminology (such as entity, value object, or aggregate) at the enterprise solution architecture level.

In the agile ESA, the *Domain Element* can apply to both application and technical areas. The domain is largely used to reduce architectural complexity, following service-orientation philosophy. Practically, when adopting the service-oriented application modernization approach, DDD, or microservice architecture, it's best to clarify domains initially from an overall monolithic system's perspective.

# 3.8 Assistive Representation Elements

Some of the core elements can have assistive visual representations for specific content expression, allowing model flexibility. The common usage association of assistive representation is shown in Table 18.

| Assistive Representation | Associated Element |
|---|---|
| Virtual Service | Non-IT services |
| Cloud Service | *System, Middleware, Node*, etc. |
| Product | All elements with *Product* property |
| DB Store or Database | *Middleware* |
| Mobile Device | *System/Device* |
| Multiple Instances | All structural elements |

---

[51] Service-oriented Methodology and Architecture
[52] Domain De-composition Method

| Assistive Representation | Associated Element |
|---|---|
| Composite Service or Process | *Application Logic Service* |

Table 18: Assistive Representation Elements

# 3.8.1 Cloud Service Element

Simple definition:

A *Cloud* (CL) is a particular area of computer system capabilities and resources available on-demand, independent of its location.

The cloud or XaaS/cloud-based service is a special type of service expressed using the cloud symbol. The *Cloud Service Element* (or *Cloud Element* for short), more about architecture than technology, meshes well with the IT service-based approach. Referencing CCA/CCRA,[53] the typical cloud services (independent of their geographic location) are defined in Table 19.

| Cloud Service | Related to | Explanation |
|---|---|---|
| SaaS (Software as a Service) | *System Element* | Providing application offering services which are supported by both software and hardware |
| PaaS (Platform as a Service) | *Middleware Element* | Providing remote middleware offering services |
| IaaS (Infrastructure as a Service) | *Node Element* | Providing infrastructure offering services including storage and networks, and predominantly node services |
| Internet Service, Network Service, etc. | *Domain Element* | Generic internet service provided by ISP,[54] remote network service, or middleware platform service |

Table 19: Typical Cloud Platform Service

Unlike the cloud, *virtualization*, which also represents virtual resource management, means a piece of middleware, a platform, an environment, a virtual node, a virtual network, or a virtual service. For cloud services, virtual resources need to be allocated

---

[53] Cloud Computing Architecture/Cloud Computing Reference Architecture
[54] Internet Service Provider

into centralized pools, which need to be orchestrated by management and automation software. Clouds deliver added benefits of self-service access, automated infrastructure scaling, dynamic resource pools, pay by usage, and so on. The agile ESA does not specify a virtualization element per se, and this effectively eliminates haziness and ambiguity.

When architecting a *cloud-native* solution, pay attention to the following:

— Refer to the Cloud-Native Architecture and take advantage of the cloud platform's automation capability, including CI/CD,[55] monitoring, fault-tolerance, scaling, and elastic infrastructure.
— Use the hosting service, managed service, and *service mesh* to save time and cost, if any.
— Take a *thorough consideration of security at the service level*, not just the system boundary, to survive the architecture in the robust-yet-fragile internet environment.
— Architect for *technical and domain changes* and design *stateless* service components for easy scalability.

When choosing a cloud deployment solution, the same architectural considerations need to be addressed. Likewise, the strength of the cloud services (such as availability and security), replaceable resources, network latency, cloud service offering scope (service catalog), level of support, TCO,[56] and especially cloud service compliance and restriction need to be considered.

# 3.8.2 Product Element

Simple definition:

A *Product* (PD) is a piece of physical software, equipment and the like offered as a whole.

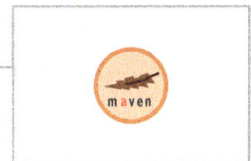

The *Product Element* is shown either in a shadow shape or in an image (if available) and

---

[55] Continuous Integration/Continuous Delivery
[56] Total Cost Ownership

can be represented from the "product" property of the associated element. Note that the product can also be treated as a composite business offering.

# 3.8.3 Application Element

Simple definition:

An *Application* (AP) is a piece of software deliverable in association with end-user distribution package(s).

An *Application Element* stems primarily from the user perspective and may contain multiple packages or be part of a package. An application contains different functional services (GUI, application logic, data, or technical). Note that a fit-for-purpose application has optimized UX for devices and persona.

# 3.8.4 Mobile Device Element

Simple definition:

A *Mobile Device* (MD) is a computing appliance that is not fixed in one location.

A *Mobile Device Element* (or *Handheld Computer Element*), similar to a system element, encloses both hardware and software pieces.

A mobile device is sometimes featured with wireless access capability. An IoT[57] device, broadly defined, is part of the mobile devices.

Note that mobile devices often require management software to meet mobile platform-specific requirements, which can be embodied in its element properties.

---

[57] Internet of Thing

# 3.8.5 DB Store Element

Simple definition:

A *DB Store* (DB) is a repository for storing and managing collections of data persistently.

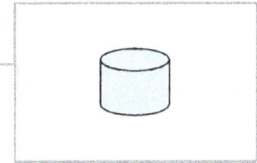

The *DB Store Element* can take several forms. Generally, a database or data warehouse is regarded as a *Middleware Element*, a *System Element*, or data storage. At the same time, a DB store in association with functional services is deemed as *backbone* data or data service. DB stores are influenced by several NFR factors: data queries, throughput, currency, consistency, size, availability, and latency. A DB store's predominant presence in architectural design is mostly shown in a familiar DB symbol for easy recognition.

# 3.8.6 Composite/Process Service Element

Simple definition:

A *Composite Service* (PS) represents multiple contained services or a process service.

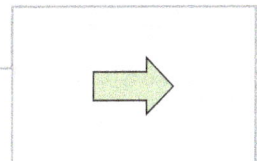

A *Composite Service Element* (or *Composite/Process Element*) is commonly associated with business logic, service logic, or control logic that usually requires choreography and/or orchestration.

# 3.8.7 Virtual Service Element

Simple definition:

A *Virtual Service* (VS) is not a physical IT service or without a clear interface.

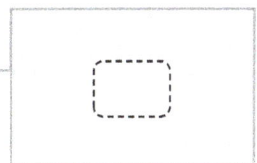

A *Virtual Service Element* is expressed using a dotted or dash line service shape, as seen from the typical example in Table 20. A virtual service can be materialized by an *Extension Element*, such as a defined *Template* for IaaC.[58]

| Virtual Service | Description | Icon Shape |
|---|---|---|
| Node | A virtual node, usually as a container. | |
| Network | Software defined network environment | |

Table 20: Typical Virtual Platform Service

# 3.8.8 Extension Element

Simple definition:

An *Extension* (EX) is a flexible representation for model element addition.

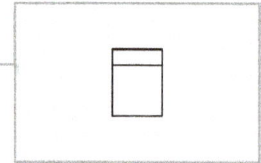

The *Extension Element* can be represented with an image, shape, or stereotype indication (see examples in Table 21).

The extension elements, not part of the enterprise solution elements per se, are generally assistive for exemplar design and implementation guidance or a better understanding of the solution context.

Notably, *Non-IT Things,* such as facility (building, kiosk, call center, and warehouse), are not essential. They do not directly impact enterprise solution architecture.

| Usage | Type | Description | Stereotype |
|---|---|---|---|
| File & Medium | Generic file | A physical file of generic nature | 《file》 |
| | Source | A source file that can be compiled into an executable file | 《source》 |
| | Library | A group of files or repository | 《library》 |
| | Framework | A well-defined non-operable | 《framework》 |

---

[58] Infrastructure as a Code

| Usage | Type | Description | Stereotype |
|---|---|---|---|
| | | reference work | |
| | Table | A database table file | 《table》 |
| | Class | A class file | 《class》 |
| | Document | A generic file, including document and text source | 《document》 |
| | Template | A template file, other than a «source» file | 《template》 |
| | Renderer | A profile, filter or plugin | 《renderer》 |
| | Screen/Page | A display screen or web page that constitutes GUI element | 《screen》 |
| | Browser | A browser on applications, PC or laptop | 《browser》 |
| | Installation | Installation medium | 《installation》 |
| Service Action | Event | A notable occurrence at a particular point in time | 《event》 |
| | Interaction | An interaction capturing exchanges of operation signatures | 《interaction》 |
| | Collaboration | A collaboration defining a set of relationships | 《collaboration》 |
| Non-IT Thing | Facility | Building, kiosk, etc. | 《facility》 |
| | Equipment | Machine, printer, etc. | 《equipment》 |
| | Material | Battery, cable, etc. | 《material》 |
| | Vehicle | Truck, etc. | 《vehicle》 |

Note:
— The flexible extension elements are chosen or created based on the solution needs. Some stereotypes (such as *Source*) are more concerned with software engineering and are not the agile ESA's primary concern.
— See Figure 11 for an exemplary visual representation of the <<screen>> extension.
— To avoid nitty-gritty details and potential confusions, software design modeling terms such as UML's *Object* are intentionally left out.

Table 21: Examples of Common Extension Elements

# Chapter 4  An A-ESA Case Study

Architectural modeling helps apply various techniques, one crucial of which is abstraction (somewhat like a black-box effect), a major distinction from the design and a must-have skill for architects. This chapter goes through a project setting to see how the techniques make sense in the modeling process.

In this chapter, the case study, based on real projects, demonstrates how to apply the various architectural elements mentioned in the early chapters. It's not meant to present a full spectrum, cluttered architectural design. Rather, the case is intentionally much more *simplified*, just enough to track the salient aspects of the key considerations. In other words, the deliverable motivation is on the usage of architectural elements, *not* the business rationale or the technical accuracy.

As architectural modeling is an iterative process that incorporates many views from incongruent viewpoints, the case walkthrough presents an *initial* work-in-progress (WIP) deliverable requiring further elaboration and modification.

# 4.1 Case Background

The case is about BRS, a retail business established in the '80s. It comprises of grocery stores and online web sales. The recent economy is driving the corporation to restructure its IT architecture to meet its mobile needs and to adopt a suitable IT expense model (OPEX[59] or CAPEX[60]). As part of the business plan for a new retail model, BRS is expanding its business to sell non-grocery items through disparate channels to create a single shopping experience.

BRS's current IT system was built in a simple three-tier architectural style, and its IT team does a lot of "fire-fighting" troubleshooting on a daily basis. It does not yet have a dedicated architect team, and its CTO takes the brunt of the major architectural responsibilities. Table 22 is an interview recap with the BRS CTO.

| Topic Area | Current Status | Issues or Needs |
|---|---|---|
| IT Strategic Plan | — Conducted an IT assessment, and identified three key issues<br>— Planned 3 year roadmap for technical changes | — Obsolete technologies from commercial systems (Solaris, Forms v3 from Oracle, etc.)<br>— Low network bandwidth (adequate today), but when applying mobile solutions, what will be a better network choice?<br>— Communication between the business and IT group generally not good |
| Enterprise Architecture (EA) | — Produced some graphic architecture diagrams<br>— Drafted lots of EA governance documents<br>— Leveraged the Retail Reference Architecture and created an initial business capability framework<br>— Employed the CAPEX Model (Corp likes to move to OPEX or a mixed model) | — Lack of deep thinking of the target architecture; without a clear enterprise architecture<br>— Need to move from traditional to more user-focused approach, matching capability framework<br>— IT transformation goals: simplification toward service-orientation<br>— Need more integrated solutions |
| Application Architecture | — Built on a web-based solution<br>— Tailored with a customizable process engine (but not designed for the mobile solution) | — Need to determine how to go mobile<br>— Need a flexible arch style for innovative applications<br>— Need a consistent user experience across all touchpoints, moving |

---

[59] OPEX (operational expenditure) is the money a company spends on an ongoing, day-to-day basis to run a business or system. [whatis.com]

[60] CAPEX (capital expenditure) is the money invested by a company to acquire or upgrade fixed, physical, non-consumable assets, such as a building, a computer, or a new business. [whatis.com]

| Topic Area | Current Status | Issues or Needs |
|---|---|---|
| | | toward digital enterprise |
| Data Architecture | — Scaled vertically, using one single catalog, and one single DB<br>— Home-made MDM, currently focusing only on hyper markets channel | — Need one central data warehouse, with lots of flexibility in catalog or item management<br>— Missing something like Hadoop, but not a priority<br>— Need operational data for channel hopping |
| Technical Architecture | — Operated with a traditional infrastructure design (virtualization not leveraged yet) | — Need workload considerations (don't have good capacity planning yet)<br>— No business continuity plan yet, which is a major concern<br>— Need an end-to-end monitoring |
| Security | — Had an intrusion test in place<br>— Provided basic customer and financial data protections | — Need to have a strong transmission security<br>— Need a very strong intrusion prevention solution |

Table 22: Interview Recap Notes with the CTO

BRS's IT strategic plan, with exhaustive background info and requirements (including user and volume scope), has been reviewed and is well documented. Now, solution architecture guidance and modeling are in order. The solution will be divided into three stages. The first stage focuses on the order processing system/solution (OPS) as a pilot project in a chosen location area, using the company's current fulfillment capabilities and interfaces for vendors and payments.

BRS invited a savvy IT consulting team to review and renovate its solution architecture by using a simple yet pragmatic modeling approach.

# 4.2 Solution Architecture Views

Visualization is key to architectural modeling. As the saying goes, a picture is worth a thousand words. Let's depict the OPS solution architecture via views, elements, and properties in a self-explanatory fashion. An enhanced solution architecture through agile governance is discussed in Chapter 5. For viewing effect, descriptions in the diagram views are intentionally kept short.

# 4.2.1 Enterprise Capability Area

This area demonstrates the BRS enterprise capability model that guides and syncs with the OPS solution building blocks.

## 4.2.1.1 Capability View – Level 1

Figure 25 shows the level 1 capability of the retail business reference components in the enterprise architecture.

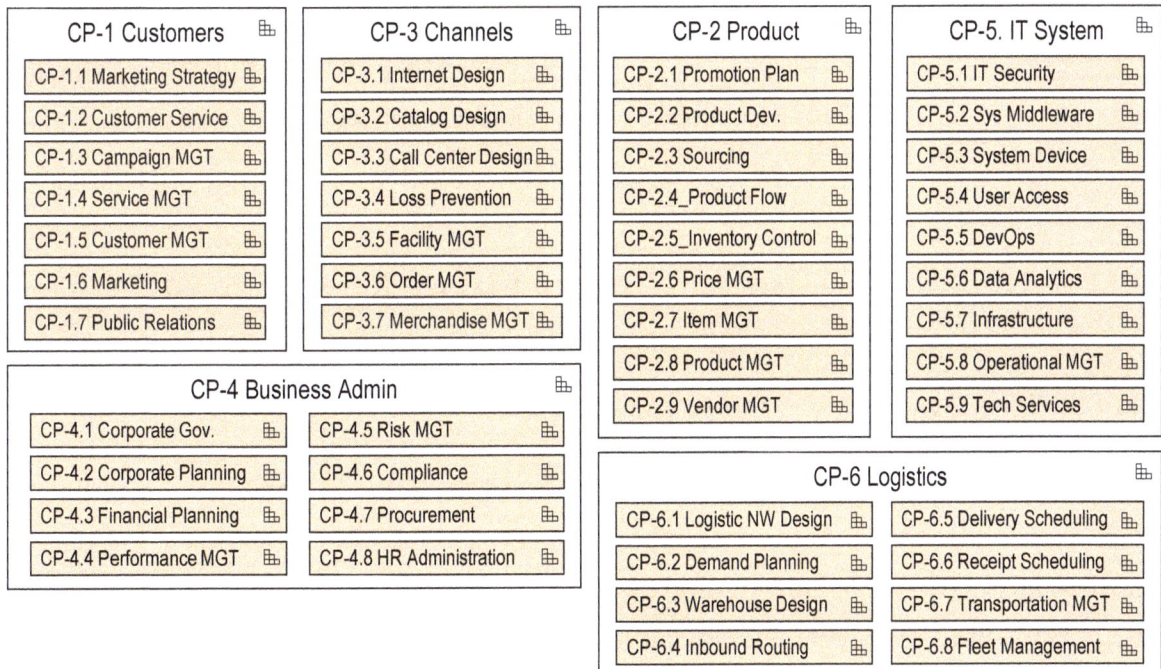

| CP-1 Customers | CP-3 Channels | CP-2 Product | CP-5. IT System |
|---|---|---|---|
| CP-1.1 Marketing Strategy | CP-3.1 Internet Design | CP-2.1 Promotion Plan | CP-5.1 IT Security |
| CP-1.2 Customer Service | CP-3.2 Catalog Design | CP-2.2 Product Dev. | CP-5.2 Sys Middleware |
| CP-1.3 Campaign MGT | CP-3.3 Call Center Design | CP-2.3 Sourcing | CP-5.3 System Device |
| CP-1.4 Service MGT | CP-3.4 Loss Prevention | CP-2.4_Product Flow | CP-5.4 User Access |
| CP-1.5 Customer MGT | CP-3.5 Facility MGT | CP-2.5_Inventory Control | CP-5.5 DevOps |
| CP-1.6 Marketing | CP-3.6 Order MGT | CP-2.6 Price MGT | CP-5.6 Data Analytics |
| CP-1.7 Public Relations | CP-3.7 Merchandise MGT | CP-2.7 Item MGT | CP-5.7 Infrastructure |
| | | CP-2.8 Product MGT | CP-5.8 Operational MGT |
| | | CP-2.9 Vendor MGT | CP-5.9 Tech Services |

**CP-4 Business Admin**

| | |
|---|---|
| CP-4.1 Corporate Gov. | CP-4.5 Risk MGT |
| CP-4.2 Corporate Planning | CP-4.6 Compliance |
| CP-4.3 Financial Planning | CP-4.7 Procurement |
| CP-4.4 Performance MGT | CP-4.8 HR Administration |

**CP-6 Logistics**

| | |
|---|---|
| CP-6.1 Logistic NW Design | CP-6.5 Delivery Scheduling |
| CP-6.2 Demand Planning | CP-6.6 Receipt Scheduling |
| CP-6.3 Warehouse Design | CP-6.7 Transportation MGT |
| CP-6.4 Inbound Routing | CP-6.8 Fleet Management |

Figure 25: Capability – Level 1

Table 23 lists a basic capability view property, and Table 24 displays the property description of a view element.

| View | Property | Description |
|---|---|---|
| CAP-1 | Name | Retail Capability Framework |
| | Owner | Yvonne Simon |
| | Organization | EA Group |
| | ROITarget | 10% First Year |
| | ROITarget | 50% Third Year |
| Note |||
| — A good enterprise solution not only considers its related capabilities, but also their interdependencies and the totality of enterprise capabilities. . |||

Table 23: Capability View Property

| Element | Property | Description |
|---|---|---|
| CP-3.6 | Name | Order Management |
| | Maturity Level | Weak |
| | Unique Owner | Bruce Swaski |
| | Level | 1 |
| | ResourceType | Application Logic Service |
| | Measurement | Shared Service Capability \| Reusability |

Table 24: Capability View – Element Property

# 4.2.1.2 Capability View – Level 2 and Level 3

Part of the level 2 capability is shown in Figure 26.

At level 3 of the capability view, there is more specificity in capability offering and service connotation. The level 3 capability is most often the touchpoint for use-case scenarios and IT service automation. Figure 27 shows the order management and security portion of the level 3 views. Table 25 lists an element property description from level 3.

**CP-3.6 Order MGT**
- CP-3.6.1 App User Interface
- CP-3.6.2 Functional Logic
- CP-3.6.3 Data Service

**CP-5.1 IT Security**
- CP-5.1.1 Security Operation
- CP-5.1.2 Data Security
- CP-5.1.3 Infrastructure Sec.
- CP-5.1.4 Application Sec.
- CP-5.1.5 Platform Sec.
- CP-5.1.7 Network Security

**CP-5.2 Sys Middleware**
- CP-5.2.1 Web Server
- CP-5.2.2 App Server
- CP-5.2.3 DB Server
- CP-5.2.4 ESB Server

**CP-5.7 Infrastructure**
- CP-5.7.1 Container & VM
- CP-5.7.2 Container MGR
- CP-5.7.3 Node
- CP-5.7.4 Network

**CP-5.8 Op MGT**
- CP-5.8.1 Runtime Analytics

**CP-5.5 DevOps**
- CP-5.5.1 App Design
- CP-5.5.2 Coding Quality
- CP-5.5.3 SCM
- CP-5.5.4 Auto Deployment
- CP-5.5.5 QA
- CP-5.5.6 Test Suite MGT
- CP-5.5.7 Build
- CP-5.5.8 Repository
- CP-5.7.1 Container & VM
- CP-5.7.2 Container MGR

**CP-5.9 Tech Services**
- CP-5.9.1 Web App
- CP-5.9.3 DB
- CP-5.9.4 Email
- CP-5.9.5 Mobile App
- CP-5.9.6 EDW
- CP-5.9.7 Gateway
- CP-5.9.8 ETL
- CP-5.9.9 Message Broker
- CP-5.9.10 Security
- CP-5.9.11 Deploy Package
- CP-5.9.12 Utility

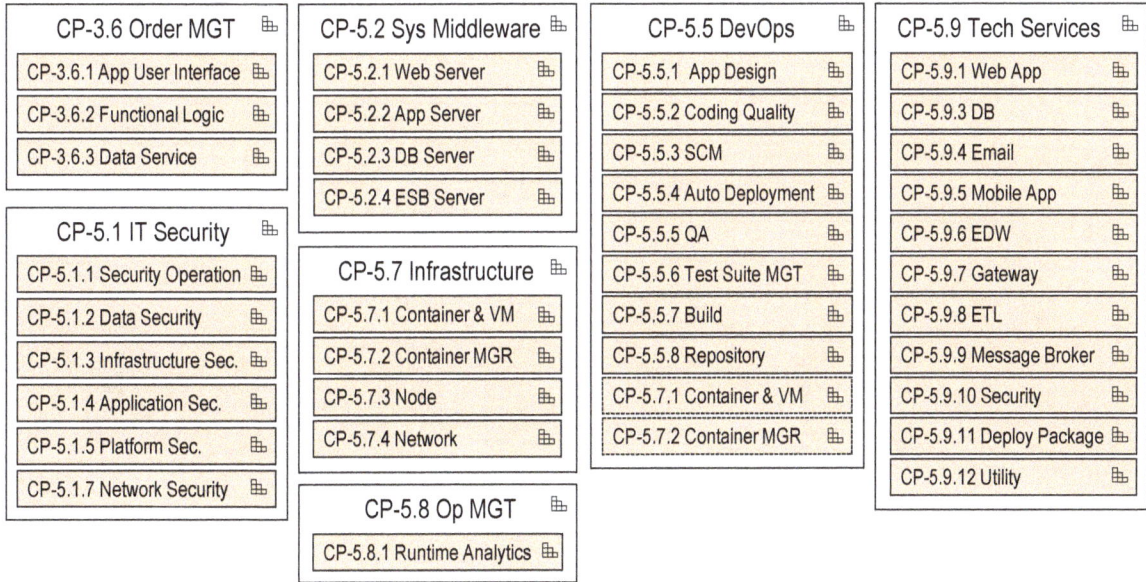

Figure 26: Capability – Level 2 (Partial)

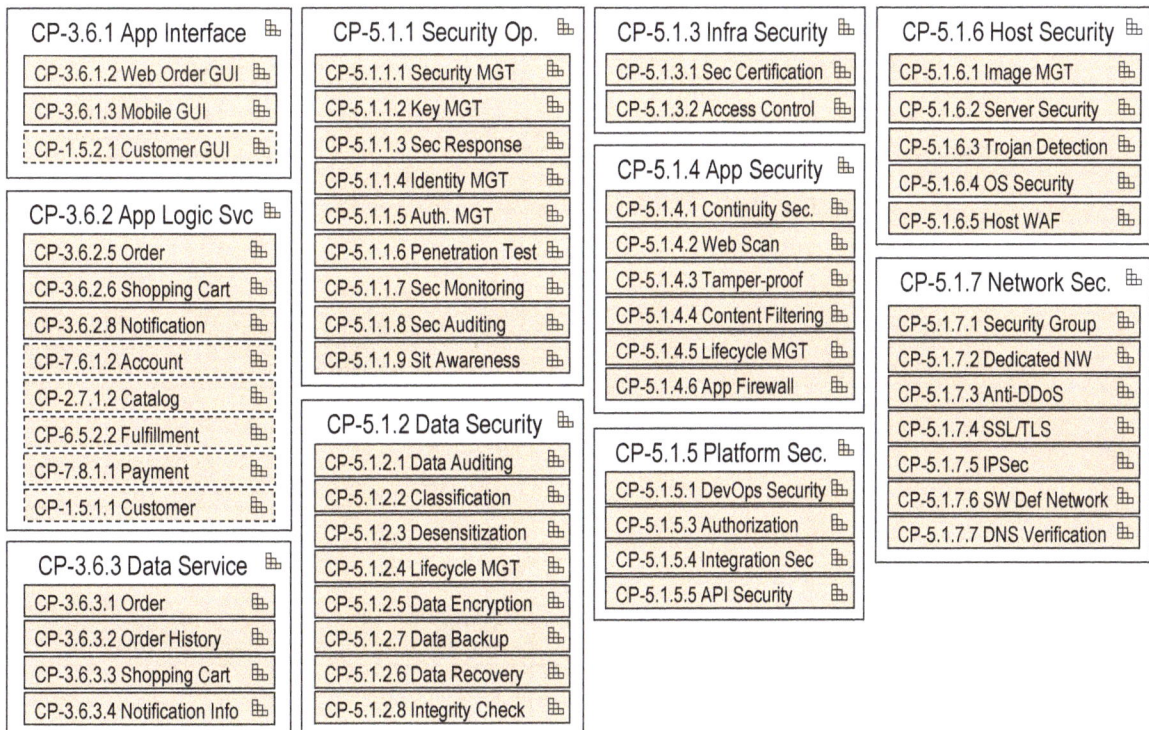

**CP-3.6.1 App Interface**
- CP-3.6.1.2 Web Order GUI
- CP-3.6.1.3 Mobile GUI
- CP-1.5.2.1 Customer GUI

**CP-3.6.2 App Logic Svc**
- CP-3.6.2.5 Order
- CP-3.6.2.6 Shopping Cart
- CP-3.6.2.8 Notification
- CP-7.6.1.2 Account
- CP-2.7.1.2 Catalog
- CP-6.5.2.2 Fulfillment
- CP-7.8.1.1 Payment
- CP-1.5.1.1 Customer

**CP-3.6.3 Data Service**
- CP-3.6.3.1 Order
- CP-3.6.3.2 Order History
- CP-3.6.3.3 Shopping Cart
- CP-3.6.3.4 Notification Info

**CP-5.1.1 Security Op.**
- CP-5.1.1.1 Security MGT
- CP-5.1.1.2 Key MGT
- CP-5.1.1.3 Sec Response
- CP-5.1.1.4 Identity MGT
- CP-5.1.1.5 Auth. MGT
- CP-5.1.1.6 Penetration Test
- CP-5.1.1.7 Sec Monitoring
- CP-5.1.1.8 Sec Auditing
- CP-5.1.1.9 Sit Awareness

**CP-5.1.2 Data Security**
- CP-5.1.2.1 Data Auditing
- CP-5.1.2.2 Classification
- CP-5.1.2.3 Desensitization
- CP-5.1.2.4 Lifecycle MGT
- CP-5.1.2.5 Data Encryption
- CP-5.1.2.7 Data Backup
- CP-5.1.2.6 Data Recovery
- CP-5.1.2.8 Integrity Check

**CP-5.1.3 Infra Security**
- CP-5.1.3.1 Sec Certification
- CP-5.1.3.2 Access Control

**CP-5.1.4 App Security**
- CP-5.1.4.1 Continuity Sec.
- CP-5.1.4.2 Web Scan
- CP-5.1.4.3 Tamper-proof
- CP-5.1.4.4 Content Filtering
- CP-5.1.4.5 Lifecycle MGT
- CP-5.1.4.6 App Firewall

**CP-5.1.5 Platform Sec.**
- CP-5.1.5.1 DevOps Security
- CP-5.1.5.3 Authorization
- CP-5.1.5.4 Integration Sec
- CP-5.1.5.5 API Security

**CP-5.1.6 Host Security**
- CP-5.1.6.1 Image MGT
- CP-5.1.6.2 Server Security
- CP-5.1.6.3 Trojan Detection
- CP-5.1.6.4 OS Security
- CP-5.1.6.5 Host WAF

**CP-5.1.7 Network Sec.**
- CP-5.1.7.1 Security Group
- CP-5.1.7.2 Dedicated NW
- CP-5.1.7.3 Anti-DDoS
- CP-5.1.7.4 SSL/TLS
- CP-5.1.7.5 IPSec
- CP-5.1.7.6 SW Def Network
- CP-5.1.7.7 DNS Verification

Figure 27: Capability- Level 3 (Order Management & Security)

| Element | Property | Description |
|---|---|---|
| CP-7.6.1.2 | Name | Account |
| | Maturity Level | Appropriate |
| | Unique Owner | Nancy Hofmann |
| | Level | 3 |
| | Service | Account Service |
| | Service | Bonus Points Service |

Table 25: Capability View – Element Property (CP-7.6.1.2)

# 4.2.2 Case Scenario Area

This area covers an order confirmation process, an order management use-case, and a page flow for order by mobile phone.

## 4.2.2.1 Process View – Order Confirmation

Table 26 exhibits a view property from the OPS process, and Table 27 is an element property description from the process. Figure 28 is an order confirmation OPS process.

| View | Property | Description |
|---|---|---|
| PRM-4 | Name | Order Confirmation |
| | Type | Business Process |
| | Role | Customer |
| | Role | Customer Representative |
| | InputData | Shopping Cart Data |
| | OutputData | Submitted Order Data |
| | KPI | Processing Time |
| | RequirementSource | Business Group | AS-IS Architecture |

Table 26: Process – View Property

| Element | Property | Description |
|---------|----------|-------------|
| TK-3 | Name | Record Payment Details |
| | Type | Task |
| | IsAtomic | Y |
| | Role | Customer Representative |
| | InputData | Payment Data |

Table 27: Process – Element Property

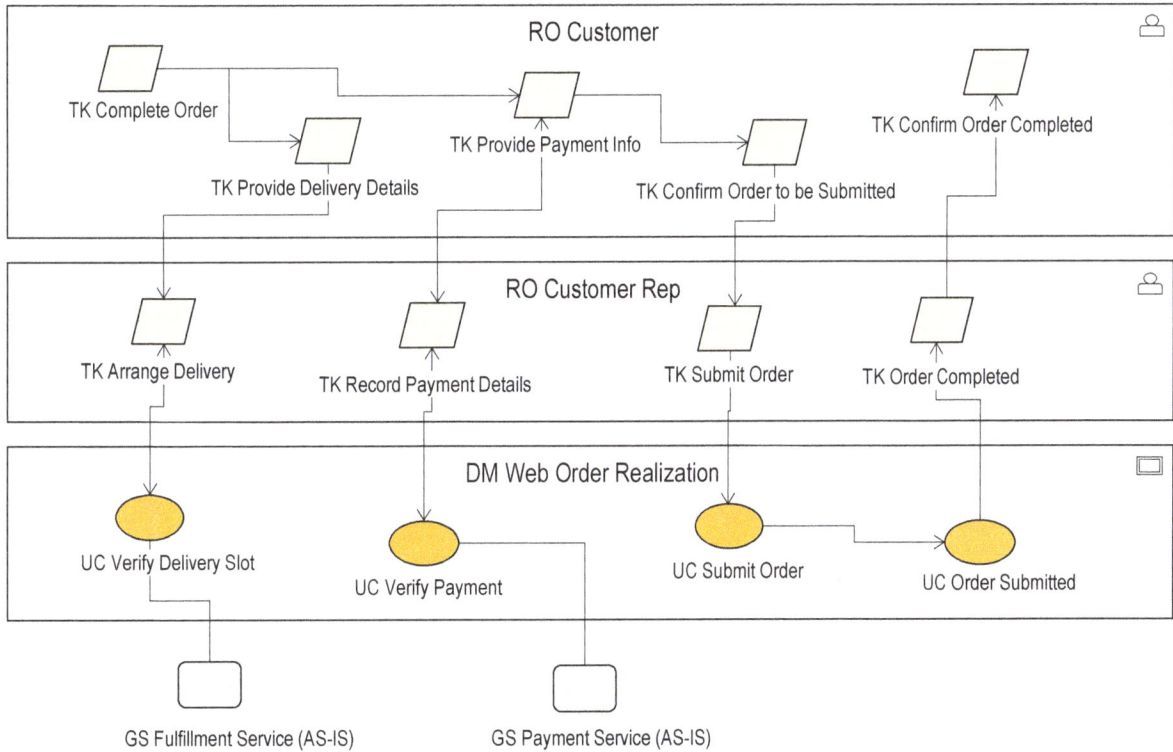

Figure 28: OPS Process View (Order Confirmation)

## 4.2.2.2 UC Model View – Order Management

Figure 29 demonstrates a use-case model view for order management. Tables 28 and 29 illustrate the property descriptions from the view and its selected elements, respectively.

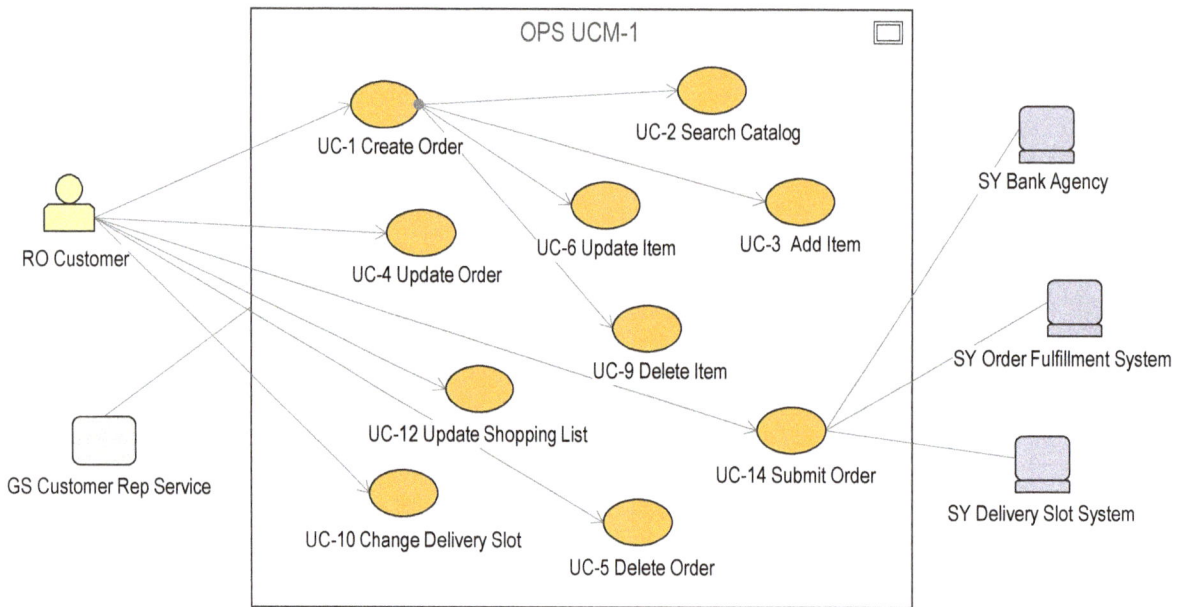

Figure 29: OPS Use Case Model View (Order Processing Management)

| View | Property | Description |
|---|---|---|
| UCM-2 | Name | Order Management |
| | Type | Use Case Model |
| | PrimaryActor | Customer |
| | SecondaryActor | System Admin |
| | BoundaryScope | OPS |
| | RequirementSource | OPS User Story.doc |

Table 28: Use Case Model View – View Property

| Element | Property | Description |
|---|---|---|
| RO-2 | Name | Customer |
| | HeadCount | 500K |
| UC-14 | Name | Submit Order |
| | Type | Use Case |
| | PreCondition | An Open Order exists |
| | SuccessOutcome | Order submitted | Order resubmitted | Order not "open" |
| | FailureOutcome | Delivery slot not available | Payment not authorized |
| | OutputDataObject | Payment Data |

Table 29: Use Case Model View – Element Property Attributes

# 4.2.2.3 Page Flow View – Order by Mobile Phone

Figure 30 shows an optional page flow view for an order by mobile phone, adhering to the KISS principle. Tables 30 and 31 exemplify the property description of the view and its elements.

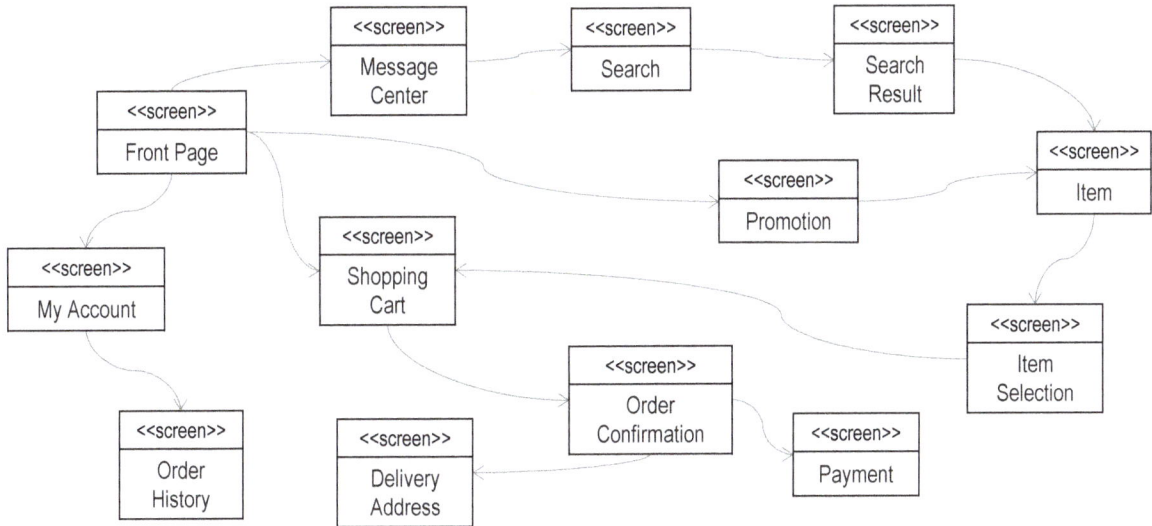

Figure 30: OPS Page Flow View (Order by Mobile Phone)

| View | Property | Description |
|---|---|---|
| PFV-1 | Name | Mobile Order |
| | Type | Page Flow View |
| | ScreenDesignProcessFlow | Conceptual Process Flow.doc |
| | OverviewofUIandScreenNav | UI and Screen Navigation.psd |
| | GraphicalUserInterfaceGuide | GUI Guidelines.docx |
| | DataServiceUsageGuide | Data Service Adapter.doc |
| | Usability | NFR.doc (Usability Section) |
| | Security | NFR.doc (Security Section) |
| | Owner | Jay Cao |
| | RequirementSource | 3/28/20 BINGO Agile Workshop |

Table 30: Page Flow View Property (Mobile Order)

| Element | Property | Description |
|---------|----------|-------------|
| EX-3 | Name | Search |
| | Type | Screen |
| | Function | Search a desired product item |
| | DataModel | Category Data Service |
| | GUIServiceAssociation | OPSMobileGUIService |
| | BusinessRule | When the Search textbox is touched, display the onscreen typewriter |
| | Comment | See the Data Service Adapter.doc for screen data manipulation details, including input source and action/implementation event. |

Table 31: Screen Element Property

# 4.2.3 Architecture Overview Area

The architecture overview area represents the solution's governing ideas and the architecture's overall building blocks. It shows the AO charts' simplified selections from the OPS solution, including the architecture block view from the solution capability perspective, the architecture solution tier view, the metrics view, and the pattern view. Together, they all form an overview of the OPS solution architecture.

## 4.2.3.1 Architecture Outline View

The OPS architecture outline view embodies both layer view and tier view.

### 4.2.3.1.1 Layer View

Figure 31 is an architecture overview pivoting on the logical solution capability of the OPS system. Tables 32 and 33 list the selected view and element properties of the OPS architecture overview. Figures 32, 33, 34, and 35 are further AO drill-downs, demonstrating how the solution capabilities are associated with UI services, application business logic services, data services, and technical services.

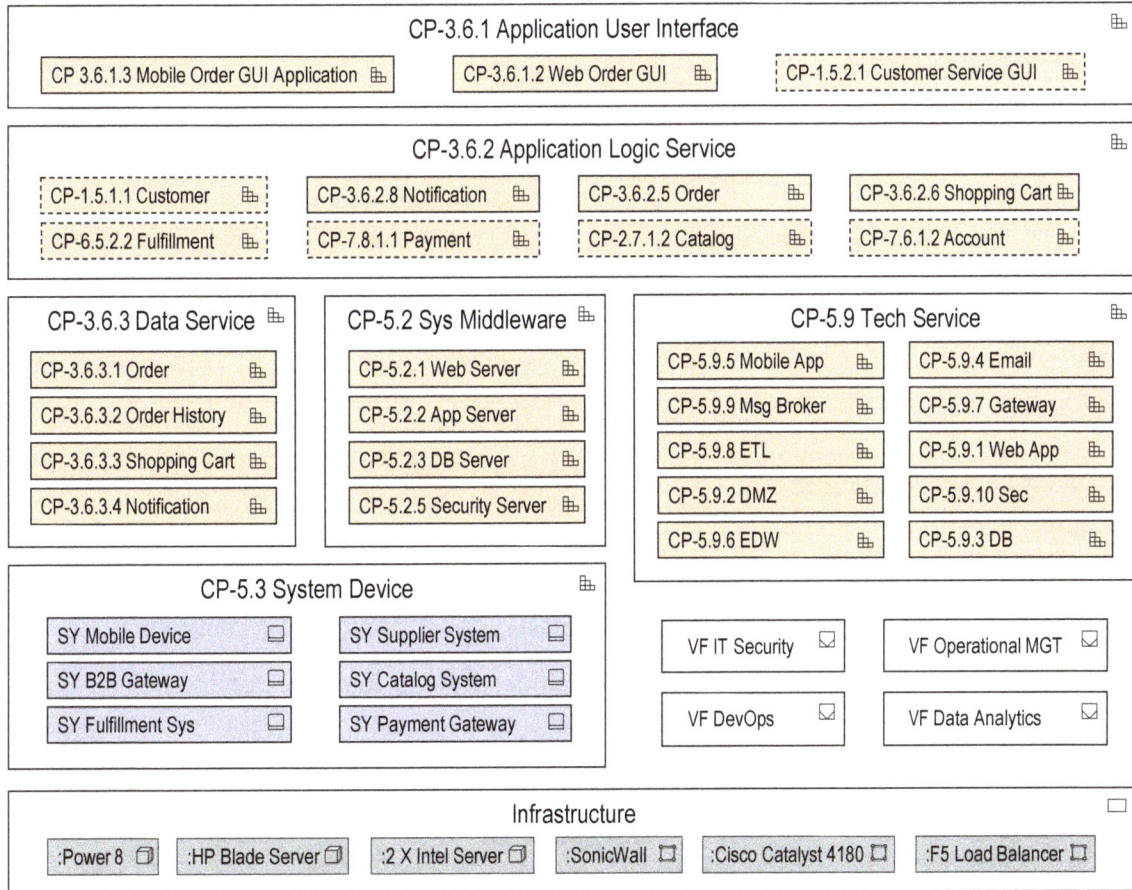

Figure 31: OPS Architecture Overview – Block View

| View | Property | Description |
|---|---|---|
| AOV-1 | Type | Architecture Overview – Layer |
| | Style | IT Service-based Architecture |
| | ArchStandard | A-ESA |
| | IsGoverningView | Y |
| | SystemContextDomain | OPS Boundary |
| | IsSketch | N |
| | ArchState | To-Be |
| | ArchStage | Phase II |
| | SolutionProject | AUC2 |
| | ProjectBudget | $1M |

| View | Property | Description |
|------|----------|-------------|
| | ProjectDuration | 03012020-01312021 |
| | CostEstimation | OPS Simulation Run.doc |

Table 32: Architecture Overview – Block View Property

| Element | Property | Description |
|---------|----------|-------------|
| VF-21 | Name | DevOps |
| | Type | View Frame |
| | Perspective | Process View |

Table 33: Architecture Overview – Element Property Attributes

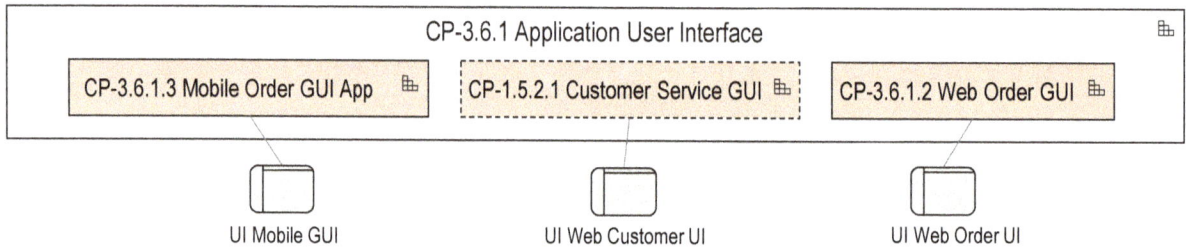

Figure 32: OPS AO – Block View Drilldown (User Interface Services)

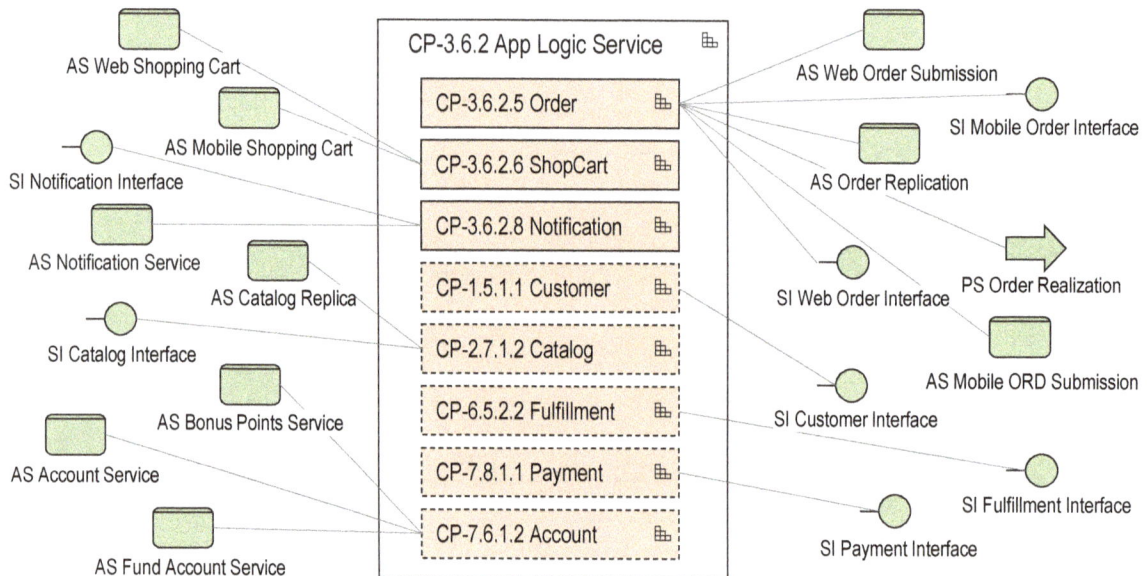

Figure 33: OPS AO – Block View Drilldown (Application Logic Services)

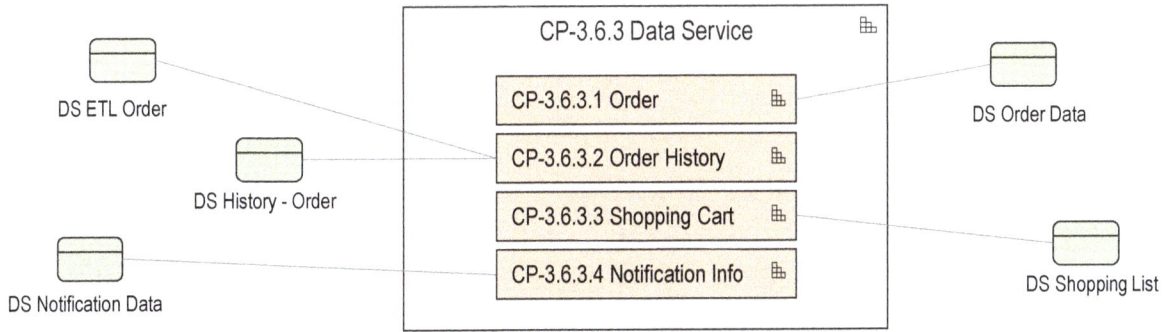

Figure 34: OPS AO – Block View Drilldown (Data Services)

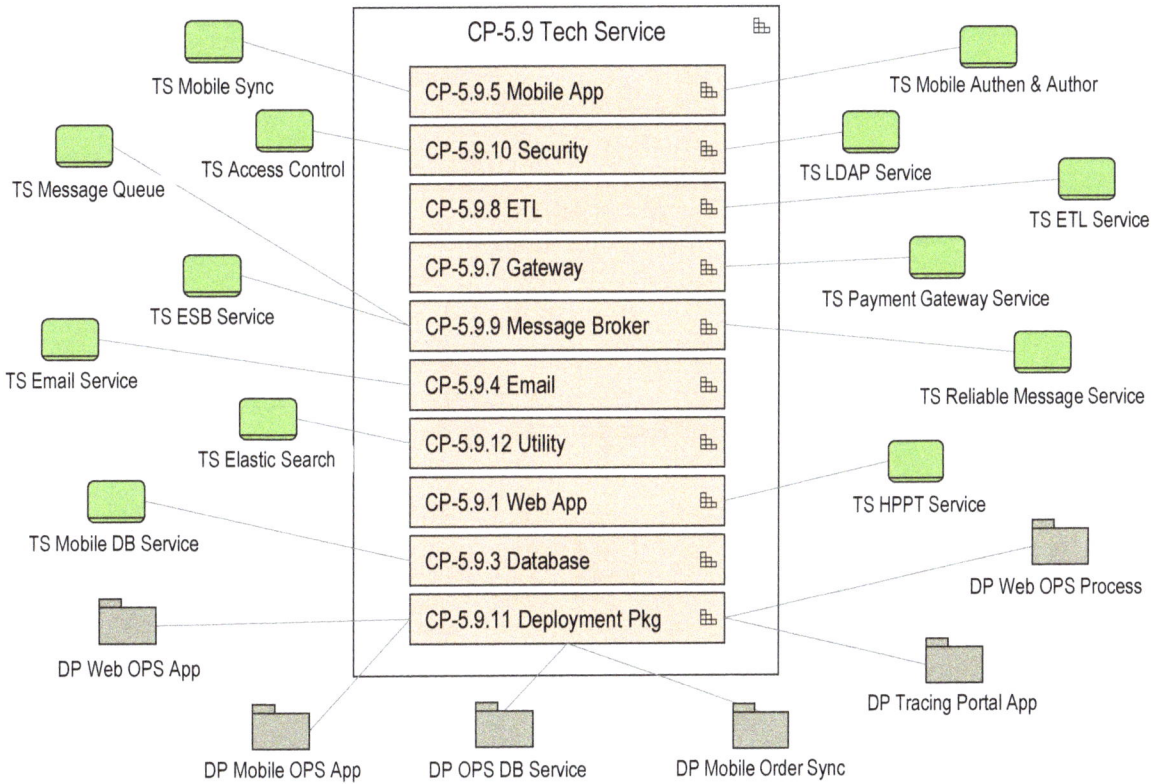

Figure 35: OPS AO – Block View Drilldown (Technical Services)

## 4.2.3.1.2 Tier View

Figure 36 is a high-level architecture tier view of the OPS system, showing an overall operational view for solution landing.

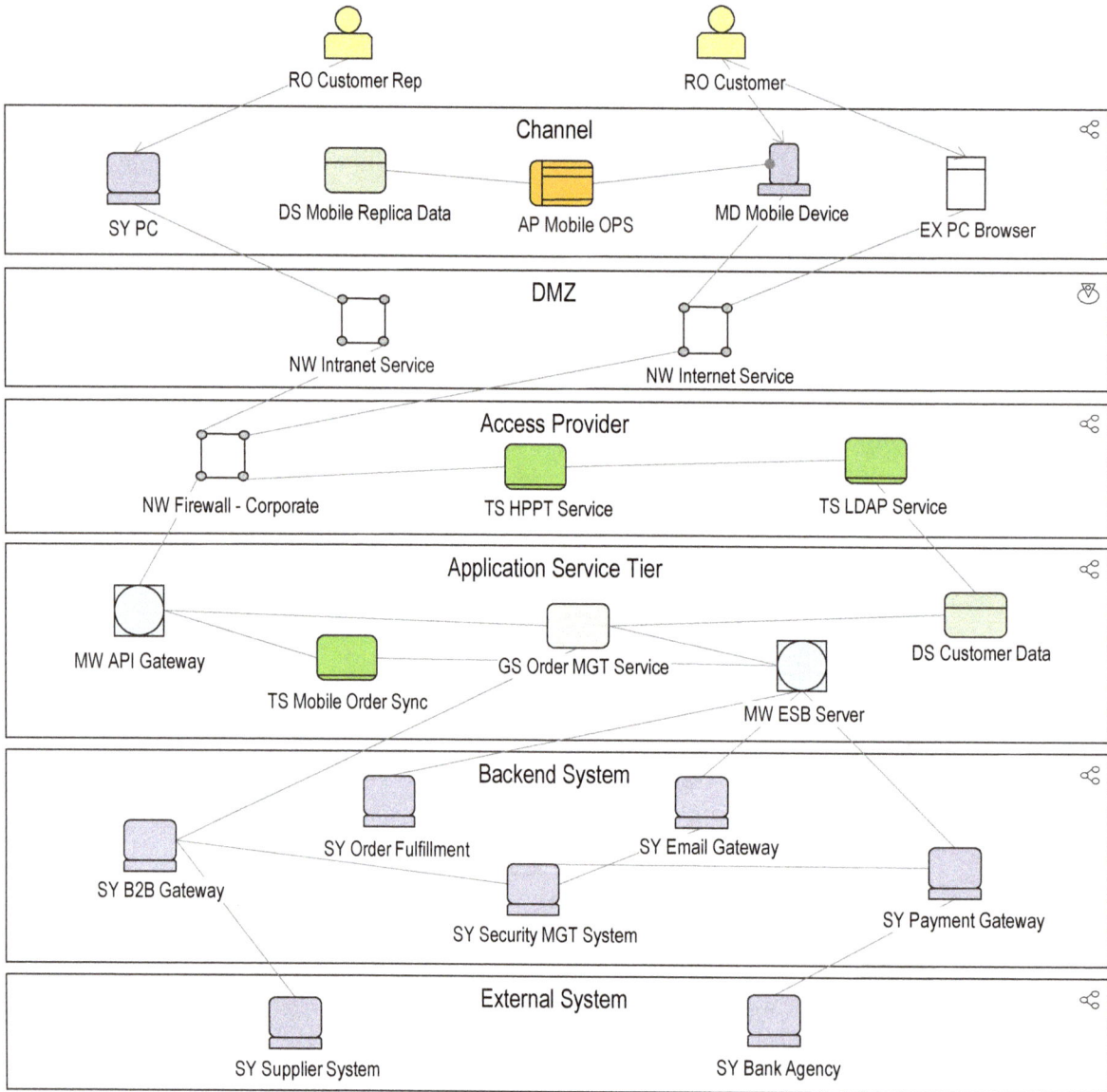

Figure 36: OPS Architecture Overview – Tier View

## 4.2.3.2 Metrics View

Figure 37 shows some of the metrics elements in the OPS project, reflecting the key architectural consideration process.

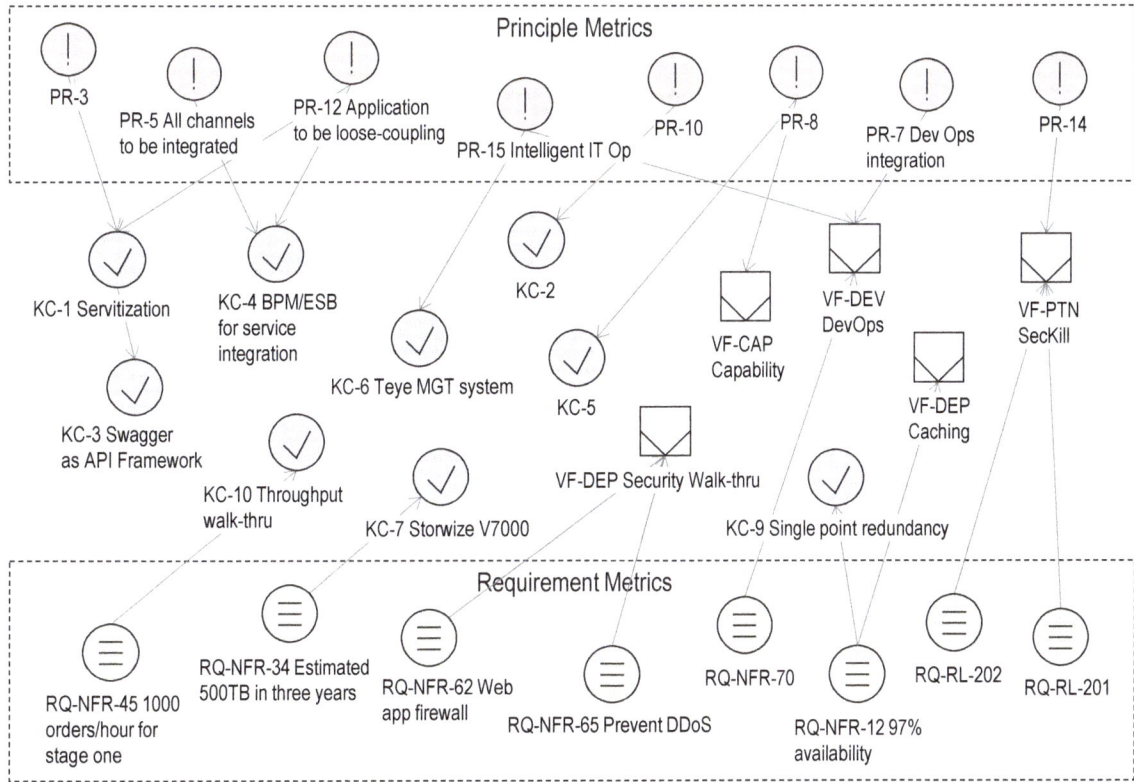

Figure 37: OPS Metrics View

Table 34 is a property description of the metrics view. Table 35 is a list of the metrics elements shown in Figure 37. Table 36 shows some of the OPS metrics elements with property attributes initially considered for the project.

| View | Property | Description |
|------|----------|-------------|
| MTR-1 | Name | OPS Metrics |
| | IsMatrixView | N |
| | InputDependency | AP \| RQ |
| | Output | KC \| RK |
| | InputFile | Metrics List.xls |

Table 34: Metrics View Property

| Element | Property Statement |
|---------|--------------------|
| KC-1 | Adopt the servitization architecture |
| KC-2 | Specify owner for each data service |
| KC-3 | Use Swagger as API Design Framework |
| KC-4 | Implement BPM/ESB for service integration |
| KC-5 | Follow domain-driven design approach |
| KC-6 | Choose operational management system-Teye |
| KC-7 | Choose Storwize V7000 as storage product |
| KC-8 | Move to public PaaS with vendor AXX as cloud platform |
| KC-9 | Eliminate redundancy for every single point of connection |
| KC-10 | Perform throughput estimation & walk-thru |
| RQ-RL-201 | Each SecKill refresh needs to reload Javascript file for the sales page |
| RQ-RL-202 | Generate new Javascript file before SecKill starts, and push it to its server |
| RQ-NFR-12 | Eliminate single-point failures and achieve 97% availability |
| RQ-NFR-34 | Estimated DB storage: 500TB in three years |
| RQ-NFR-62 | Web application security: firewall |
| RQ-NFR-65 | Prevent distributed denial-of-service (DDoS) attacks |
| RQ-NFR-70 | System should be built using a dev environment based on Java J2EE |
| RQ-NFR-45 | 1000 orders per hour for stage one solution |
| RK-5 | RTO/RPO and disaster recovery (DR) are not in place yet |
| RK-7 | More servers are needed for HA redundancy |
| RK-10 | Separate SecKill environment is needed but not ready yet |
| PR-3 | Applications follow service-orientation |
| PR-5 | All channels must be converged into a same order process |
| PR-7 | It's required to adopt development and deployment integration |
| PR-8 | Functional process needs to be compatible with the capability framework |
| PR-10 | Each data must have a unique owner |
| PR-12 | Application services need to be highly-cohesive and loosely-coupled |
| PR-14 | SecKill needs to be deployed in a separate environment |
| PR-15 | Achieve IT intelligent operation |
| Note: | |
| — KC-1 matters as it's a new architectural style for the solution | |
| — The *Risk Elements* are selectively hidden from the figure | |

Table 35: List of Metrics Elements in Figure 37

| Element | Property | Description |
|---------|----------|-------------|
| RQ-NFR-11 | Type | Non-functional Requirement |
| | Category | Availability |
| | Statement | 7x24 online presence and maintenance support |

| Element | Property | Description |
|---|---|---|
| RQ-NFR-12 | Requirement-Availability | Elimination of single-point failures to achieve 97% availability |
| RQ-NFR-40 | Requirement-Performance | Response time for browsing pages should be < 1s |
| | ValueRange | < 1s |
| | WorstValue | 15s |
| | StressCase | Black Friday Sales |
| RQ-NFR-41 | Requirement-Performance | Response time for start page should be < 8s |
| RQ-NFR-42 | Requirement-Performance | Response time for non-browsing pages should be < 3s |
| RQ-NFR-43 | Requirement-Performance | Page downloading time should be < 18s |
| RQ-NFR-44 | Requirement-Performance | 100M page hits per hour should be supported |
| RQ-NFR-45 | Requirement-Performance | 1000 orders per hour for stage one solution |
| RQ-NFR-46 | Requirement-Performance | 100k orders per hour for production |
| RQ-NFR-47 | Requirement-Performance | System should support 1M UV (unique visitor) hits during peak hours |
| RQ-NFR-48 | Requirement-Performance | 500k online users |
| RQ-NFR-49 | Requirement-Performance | 15k concurrent users |
| RQ-NFR-31 | Requirement-Capacity | Capacity 10M product SKU |
| RQ-NFR-32 | Requirement-Capacity | 500k registered customers |
| RQ-NFR-33 | Requirement-Capacity | 80M orders |
| RQ-NFR-34 | Requirement-Capacity | Estimated DB storage: 500TB in three years |
| RQ-NFR-60 | Requirement-Security | DNS security protection |
| RQ-NFR-62 | Category | Security |
| | Statement | Web application firewall |
| RQ-NFR-64 | Requirement-Security | Prevent cross site scripting (XSS) and buffer overflow |
| RQ-NFR-65 | Category | Security |
| | Statement | Prevent distributed denial-of-service (DDoS) attacks |
| RQ-NFR-66 | Requirement-Security | Prevent cross-site request forgery (CSRF) |
| RQ-NFR-74 | Requirement-Usability | System changes or application updates should have no impact to user experience |
| RQ-NFR-75 | Requirement-Usability | New page style should be consistent with existing ones |
| RQ-NFR-56 | Requirement-Scalability | System should be able to support the 3 year sales target |
| RQ-NFR-54 | Requirement-Reliability | User data record will be secured with accuracy |
| RQ-NFR-50 | Requirement-Maintainability | DB back up during night-time slow hours on a daily basis |

| Element | Property | Description |
|---|---|---|
| RQ-NFR-70 | Requirement-Technical Constraint | The system should be built using a development environment based on Java J2EE. |
| RQ-RL-100 | Requirement-Rule | Update ORDERS and ORDERITEMS not from table directly but from an Order data service |
| KC-3 | Type | Key Choice |
| | Statement | API Design Framework |
| | Alternatives | 1. Swagger; 2. APICur.io |
| | Decision | Swagger |
| | Justification | Most commonly used in industry |
| | Stakeholder | Developer, Designer |
| PR-10 | ID | 10 |
| | Type | Principle |
| | Name | Unique owner |
| | Statement | Each data has a unique owner |
| | Rationale | Data is produced during business activities and recorded thereof. Data owner should be responsible for data timeliness, accuracy, completeness, and consistency, and facilitate effective management and application of its associated information. |
| | Implication | Data is owned by a business owner |
| | Implication | Each data should define a unique owner |
| | Implication | Business owner is eventually responsible for the data quality |
| | Implication | Data owner should designate a data expert to assist his/her responsibilities |
| | Level | Solution |
| | Layer | Information Architecture |
| RQ-RL-201 | Type | Requirement |
| | Category | Rule |
| | Statement | Each SecKill refresh needs to reload Javascript file for the sales product page |
| | Association | RQ-202 |
| | Comment | Follow PR-14 |
| RK-10 | Type | Risk |
| | Statement | Separate SecKill environment needed but not ready yet |
| | Association | RQ-201 | RQ-202 |
| | IssueResolution | Make an assessment of cloud vendor and |

| Element | Property | Description |
|---|---|---|
| | | platform options. See KC-100 |
| | Status | Pending |
| | Likelihood | Low |
| | Impact | High |
| | Effort | Medium |
| | Owner | Dam Quiver |
| | Deadline | TBD |
| | Priority | High |
| | Recommendation | Lease a cloud environment |
| | Assumption | CTO will readily approve the recommendation |
| | Dependency | Operation admin experienced in cloud native application environment |
| KC-8 | Type | Key Choice |
| | Statement | Cloud Platform Choice |
| | Alternatives | Public \| Private \| Hybrid |
| | Decision | Public PaaS with vendor AXX |
| | Justification | Chosen based on the criteria analysis |
| | Stakeholder | Developer, Designer |
| | Criterion | On-premise \| off-premise |
| | Criterion | SaaS \| PaaS \| IaaS |
| | Criterion | Business values |
| | Criterion | Effort including skill requirement |
| | Criterion | API maturity |
| | Criterion | Cloud affinity |
| | Criterion | Multi-tenancy |
| | Explanation | See "Cloud platform assessment and analysis report.doc" |

Note:
— It will be a long list to show all the *metrics* elements, so only part of the elements for the project is demonstrated in this table.

Table 36: Property Attributes of Metrics Elements

# 4.2.3.3 DevOps View

As recorded in the CTO interview, communication between the business and the IT group is generally not good, so the consulting architect team recommends a DevOps architecture solution. In the following sections, the DevOps view shows an environment perspective, a simple process perspective, and a perspective with images.

## 4.2.3.3.1 Environment Perspective

Figure 38 is the environment perspective of DevOps.

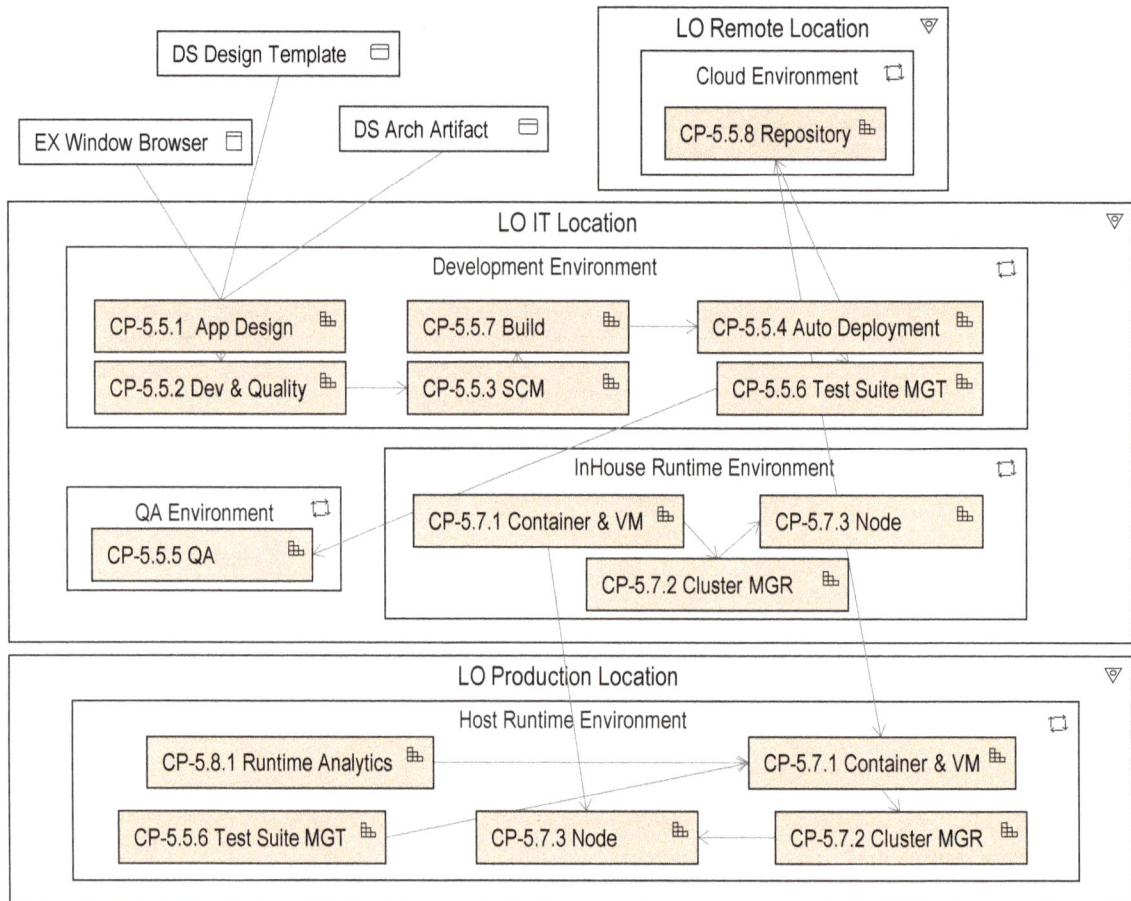

Figure 38: DevOps View – Environment Perspective

## 4.2.3.3.2 Process Perspective

Figure 39 is a DevOps process perspective, and Table 37 lists a property description of the DevOps process perspective. Figure 40 is a DevOps process with product images for the OPS solution.

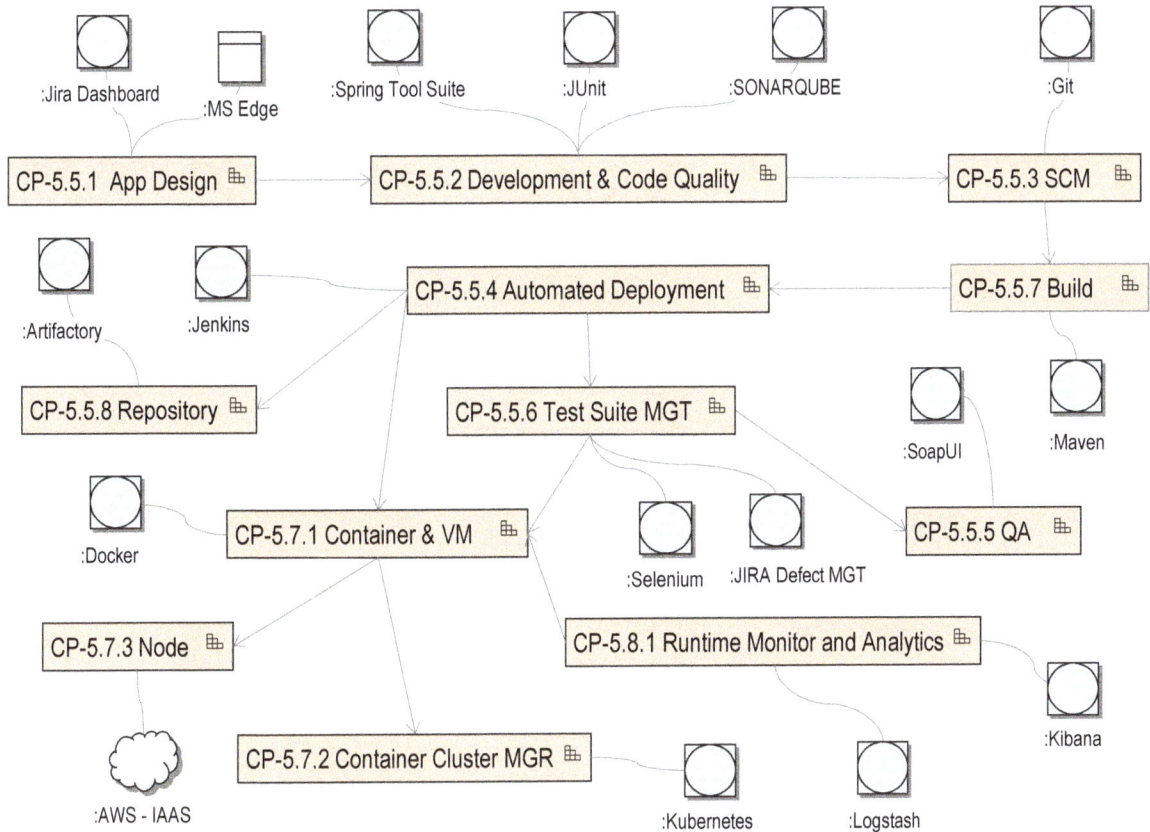

Figure 39: DevOps View – Process Perspective

| View | Property | Description |
|---|---|---|
| DEV-2 | Name | OPS DevOps Process View |
| | Type | DevOps |
| | Category | Process View |
| | SkillRequirement | Microservice Architecture |
| | SkillRequirement | Cloud Native |
| | SkillRequirement | PaaS |
| | IsSketch | N |

Table 37: DevOps View – Process View Property

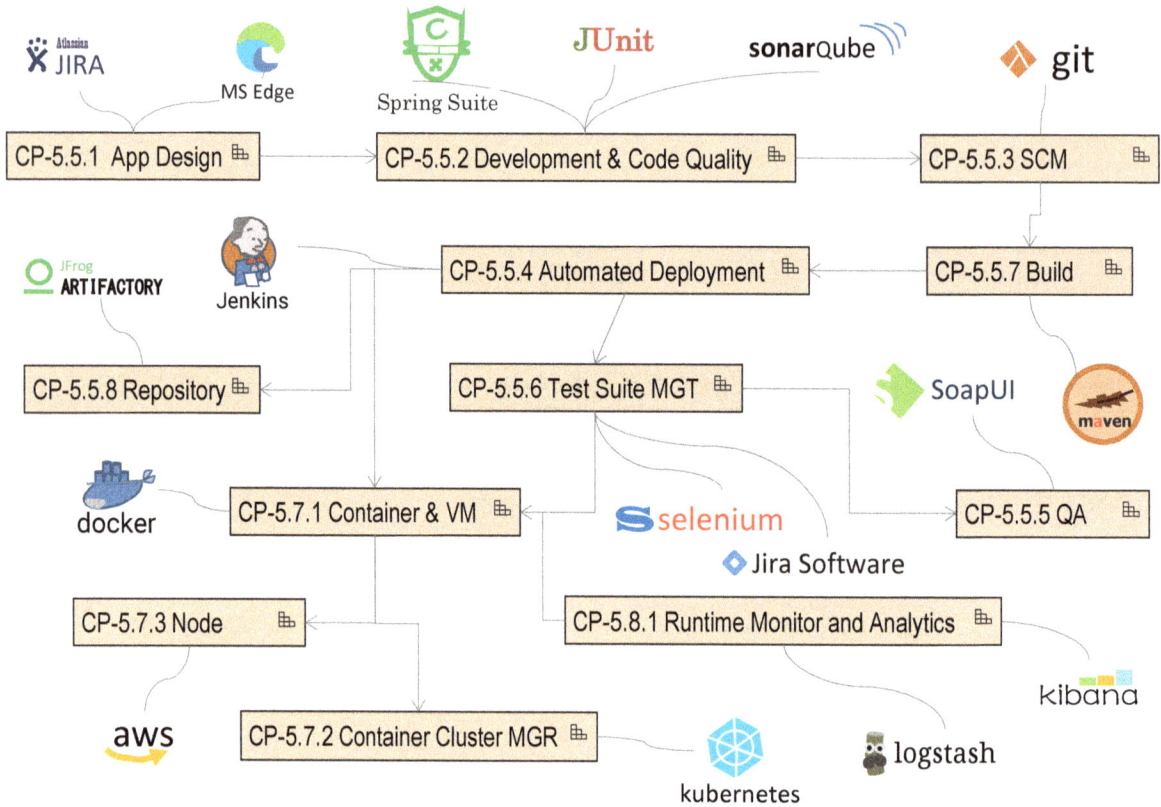

Figure 40: DevOps View – Process Perspective with Product Images

## 4.2.3.4 Pattern – SecKill

Table 38 lists a view property of the SecKill pattern. Figure 41 shows a SecKill pattern for the promotional sales days (one of the OPS project's architectural patterns).

| View | Property | Description |
|------|----------|-------------|
| PTN-3 | Name | SecKill |
| | Type | Pattern |
| | Category | Cloud Environment |
| | IsSketch | Y |

Table 38: Property of Pattern View – SecKill

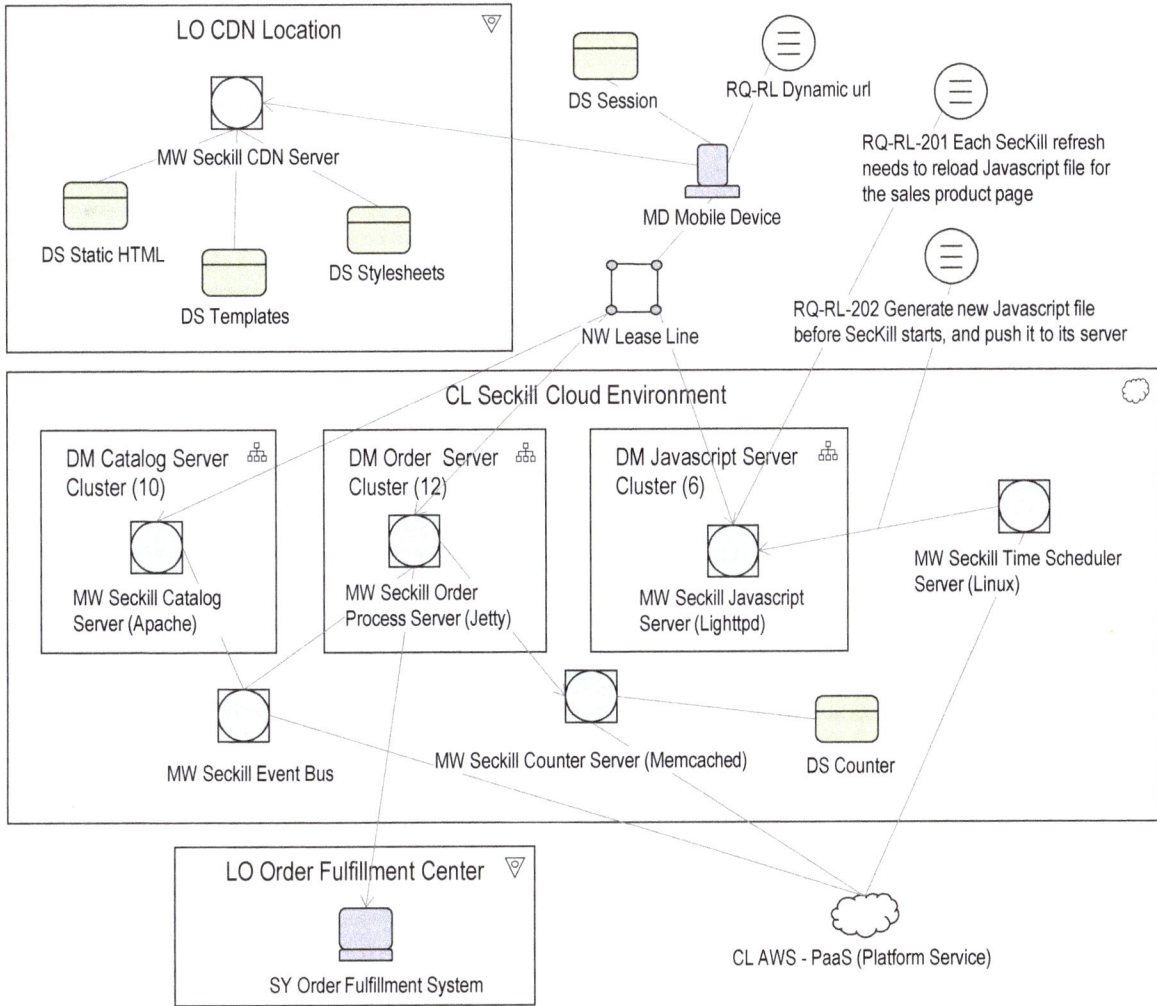

Figure 41: Pattern View – SecKill

# 4.2.3.5 Validation View

There is a long list of relationship validations automatically generated from the OPS solution tooling. Below are a couple of demonstrations.

## 4.2.3.5.1 Validation View – Data Relationship

Figure 42 shows the key OPS data service association. Table 39 is the general specification of the view property.

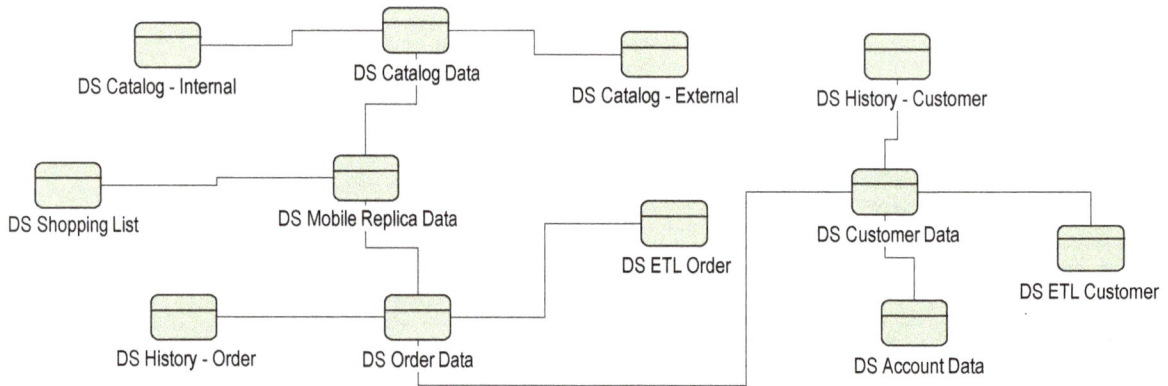

Figure 42: OPS Relationship Validation – Data Services

| View | Property | Description |
|---|---|---|
| VLD-1 | Name | Data Service Relationship |
| | Type | Validation |
| | IsMatrixView | N |
| | IsCrossCutting | Y |
| | IsWalkThru | N |
| | IsEditable | N |

Table 39: Relationship Validation – View Property

## 4.2.3.5.2 Validation View – Infrastructural Relationship

Figure 43 shows the OPS relationship validation for the nodes and networks.

Adding up the middleware elements in Figure 43, Figure 44 shows the OPS relationship validation for the nodes, networks, and middleware.

Adding up the system elements in Figure 44, Figure 45 shows the OPS relationship validation for the nodes and networks, middleware, and systems.

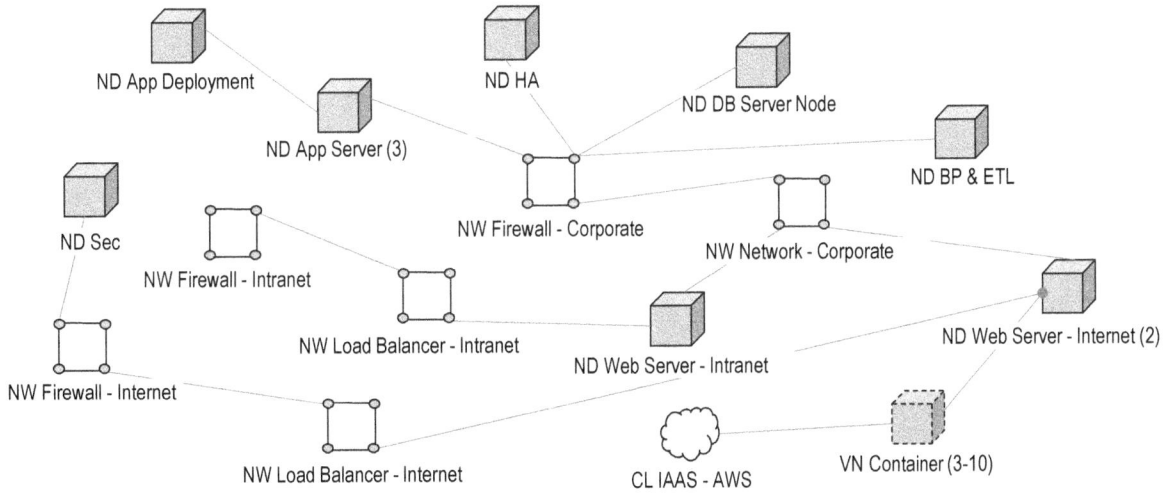

Figure 43: OPS Relationship Validation – Node and Network

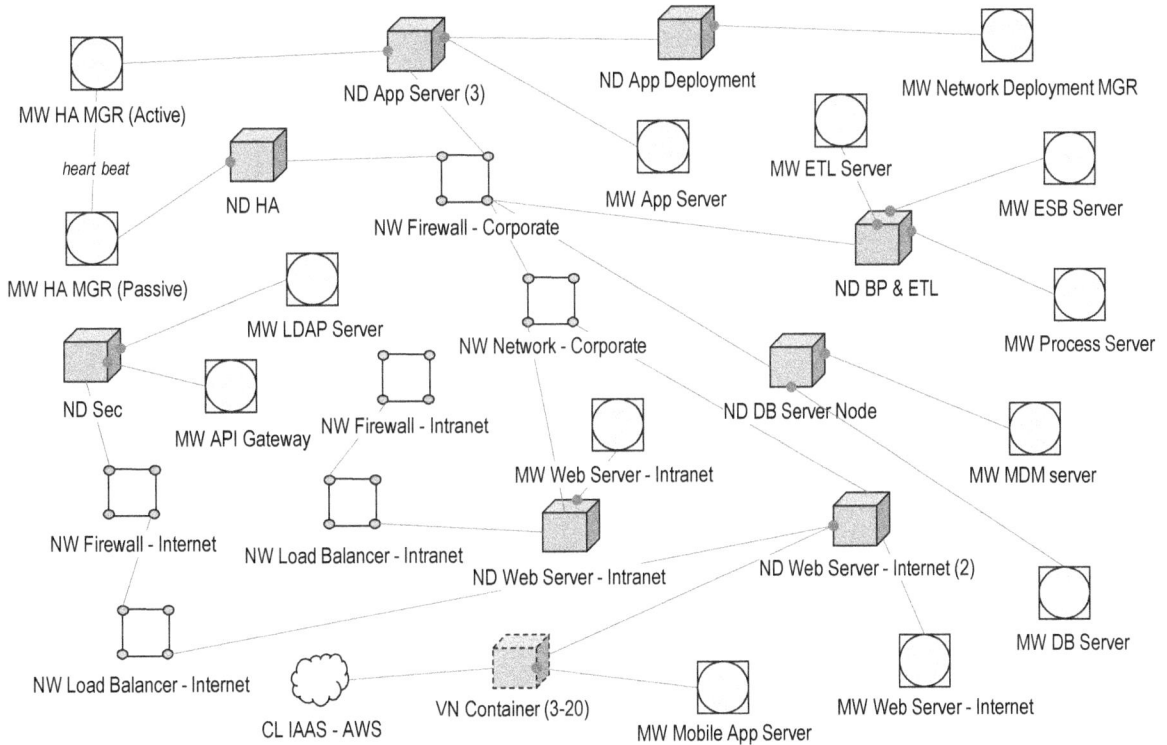

Figure 44: OPS Relationship Validation – Node, Network, and Middleware

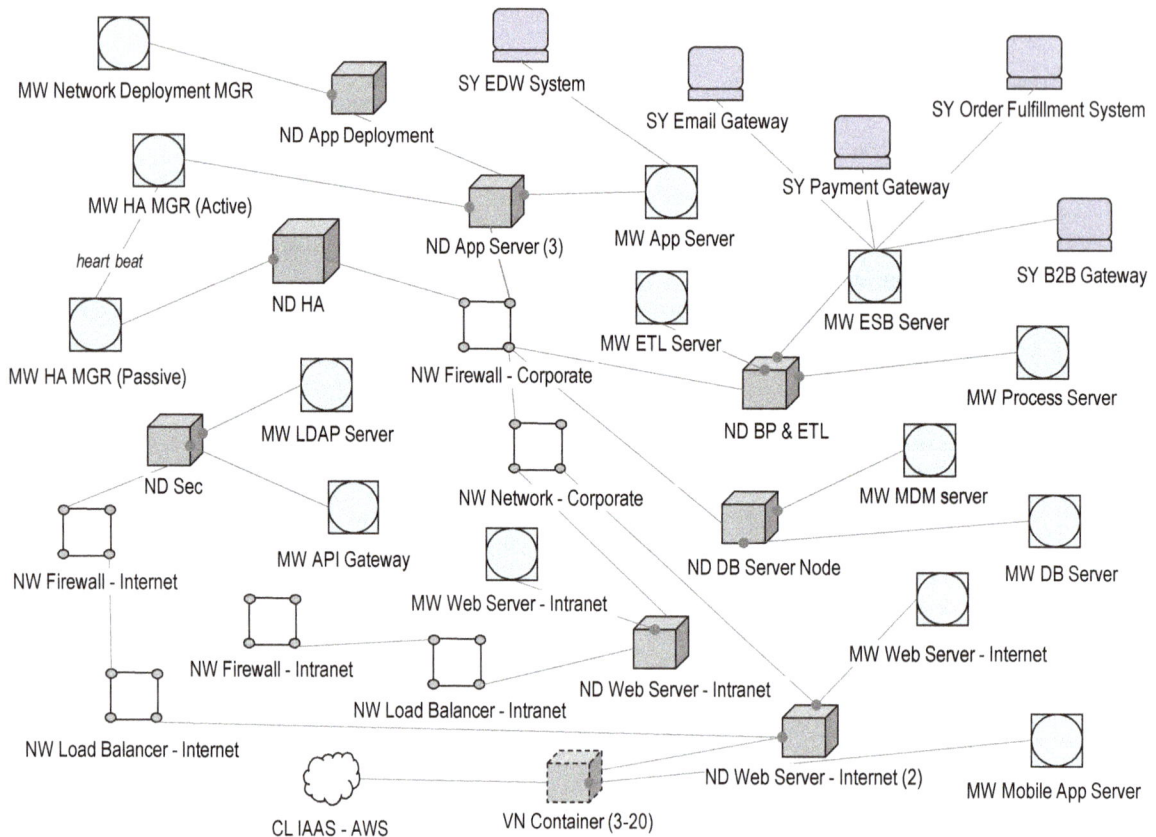

Figure 45: OPS Relationship Validation – Node, Network, Middleware, and System

# 4.2.4 Functional Area

Functional area shows typical functional interaction and relationship views from the OPS solution.

## 4.2.4.1 Service Interaction – Submit Web Order

Figure 46 is one of the service sequence interaction views for the OPS web order submission. Table 40 shows an interaction view's property attributes.

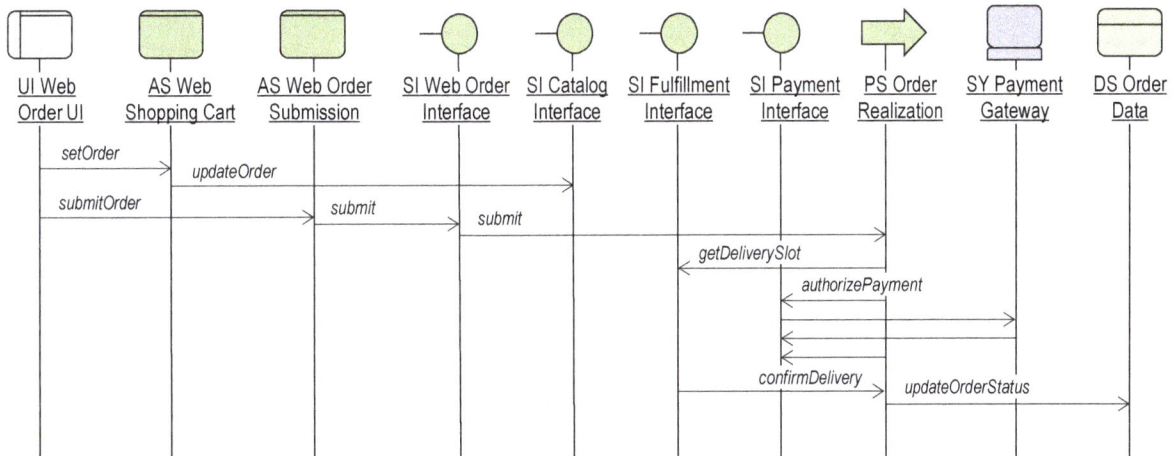

Figure 46: OPS Service Interaction View – Submit Web Order

| View | Property | Description |
|---|---|---|
| SIV-2 | Name | Submit Web Order |
| | Type | Service Interaction |
| | Category | Sequence |
| | IsProcess | Y |
| | ServiceRelationship | Order Processing System |
| | SourceUseCase | Submit Web Order |
| | TestSpec | Synthetic Testing 2 |
| | IsWalkThru | N |

Note:
— At the enterprise solution level, the design details (such as synchronous/asynchronous message, object creation/destruction, and state invariants/constraints) are not included.
— Generally, each service interaction view corresponds to a use-case.

Table 40: Interaction View Property Attributes

# 4.2.4.2 Service Collaboration – Submit Web Order

Figure 47 is virtually the same as Figure 46, presented in a collaborative format without the lifeline specification.

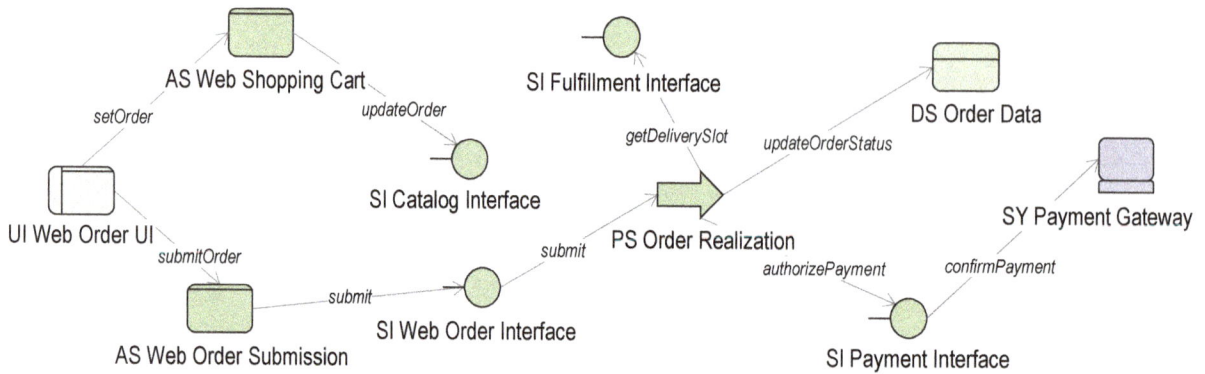

Figure 47: OPS Service Collaboration View – Submit Web Order

# 4.2.4.3 Service Relationship View – OPS

Figure 48 is the OPS service relationship view employing the layering technique.

Table 41 displays some of its element properties, exemplifying partial specifications for the four functional services and service interface.

This is the critical step for functional service specifications. The user interface elements specify the type of users, access frequency, access mechanism, concurrency, etc. The application logic service elements determine application business responsibilities, cohesion, core granularity, invocation mechanism, etc. The data service elements indicate data type, record size, data compliance, volatility, usage intensity, etc. The technical service elements decide on the realization approach, transactional execution, runtime service parametric cost, etc. The service interface elements clearly define service interface, API service, etc.

When partitioning functional services, the service relationship view generally helps apply certain key architectural techniques: layering, loose-coupling, technical isolation, and domain-based service granularity, while incorporating an architectural thinking process along with tradeoff decisions.

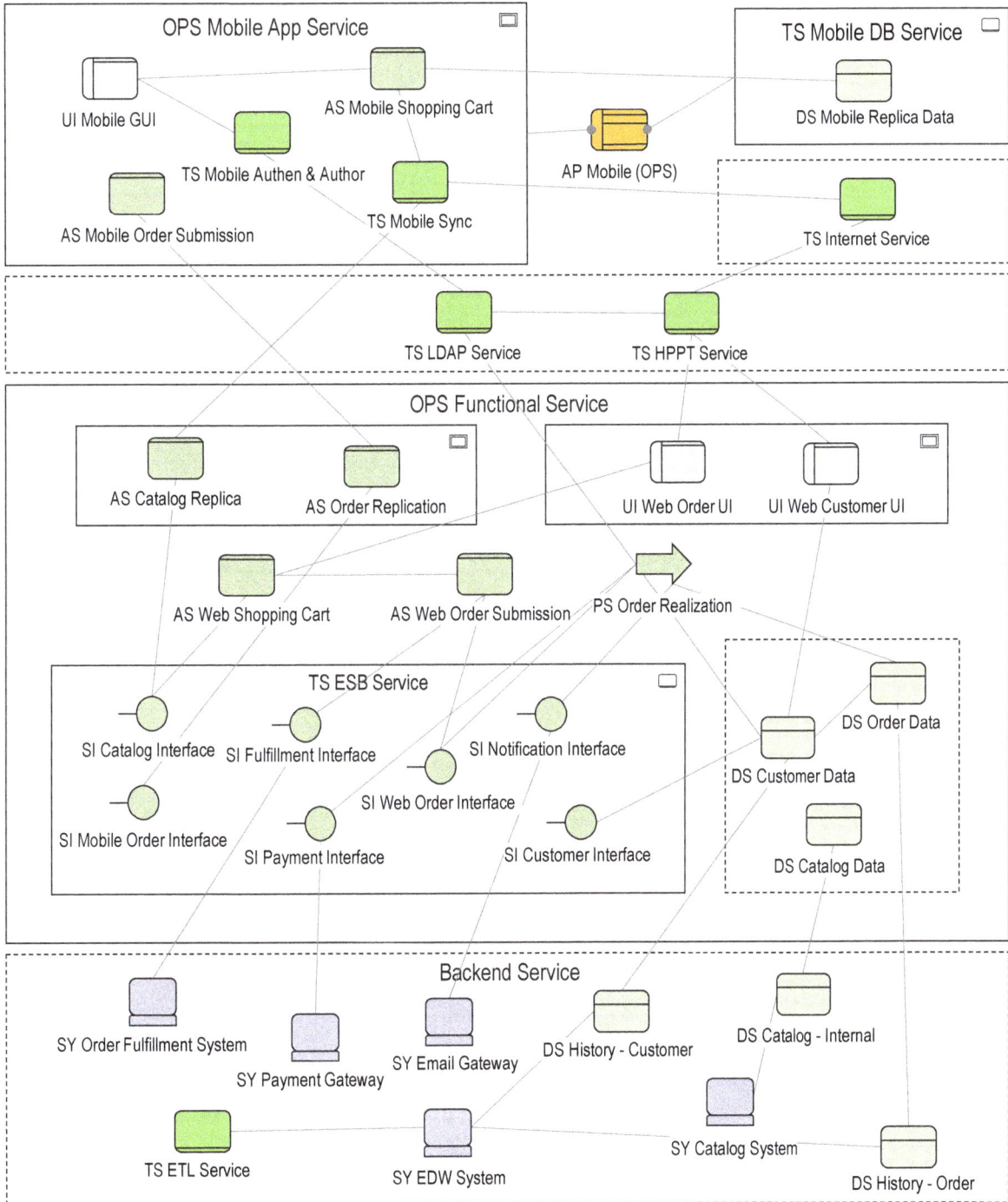

Figure 48: OPS Service Relationship View

| Element | Property | Description |
|---------|----------|-------------|
| UI-2 | Name | Web Order UI |
| | AccessFrequency | Medium |
| | InterfaceSystem | Desktop App \| Browser Plugin |
| | DesignDoc | OPS GUI Design document.do |
| | DesignTool | Axure UI \| MAUI |
| | GUIDesignStyle | Responsive |
| | TestSpec | Wireframe Test IV |
| | UserType | Naïve |
| | Concurrency | Medium |
| AS-13 | Name | Web Order Submission |
| | Type | Application Logic Service |
| | IsComposite | Y |
| | TransactionRate | High |
| | ProgrammingLanguage | Java |
| | DevTools | VS Code for Java |
| | HasDegradedFunction | N |
| | GranularityLevel | Composite |
| | SpecialSkill | DDD, SOA |
| SI-5 | Name | Web Order Interface |
| | Type | Service Component Interface |
| | TargetProtocol | jsm |
| | Scope | Private |
| | InputParameter | Order Data Service |
| | ReturnParameter | Order Data Service |
| | TestingURL | /v5/orders |
| DS-1 | Name | Order Data |
| | Type | Data Service |
| | DataFormat | Structured |
| | DataStore | Data Object |
| | IsEncrypted | Y |
| | IsAudited | Y |
| | IsArchived | Y |
| | DataItem | Order Object |
| | Volatility | High |
| | Concurrency | Medium |
| | UsageIntensity | High |
| | TransactionIntegrity | Medium |
| | DataSplit | OrderID |
| TS-4 | Name | Mobile Sync |
| | MiddlewareAssociation | None |

| Element | Property | Description |
|---|---|---|
| | TransactionType | Intermittent |
| | ProgrammingLanguage | Java |
| | RealizationApproach | Outsourcing |

Table 41: Service Relationship – Element Property Attributes

# 4.2.4.4 Service Component Realization

The service component realization is a liaison between service architecture and component implementation. It's part of the architectural validation to assure its landing feasibility. The following is a simple illustration of typical OPS realization tasks.

## 4.2.4.4.1 Service Component Interface Specification

Figure 49 illustrates the OPS service component interface specifications, showing the <<use>> (consumer) and <<offer>> (provider) of the order submission service component interface.

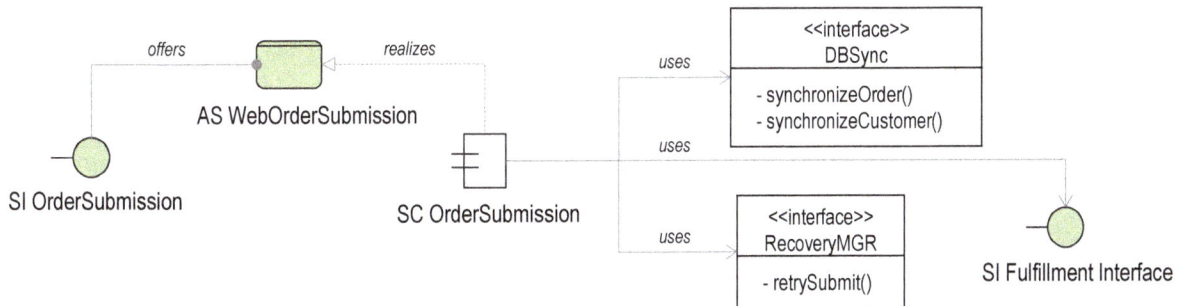

Figure 49: OPS Service Component Interface Specification

## 4.2.4.4.2 Service Component Interface Responsibility

Figure 50 indicates the OPS service component interface responsibilities, and pre- and post-conditions in <<design rule>> and operations of <<interface>> and <<class entity>>.

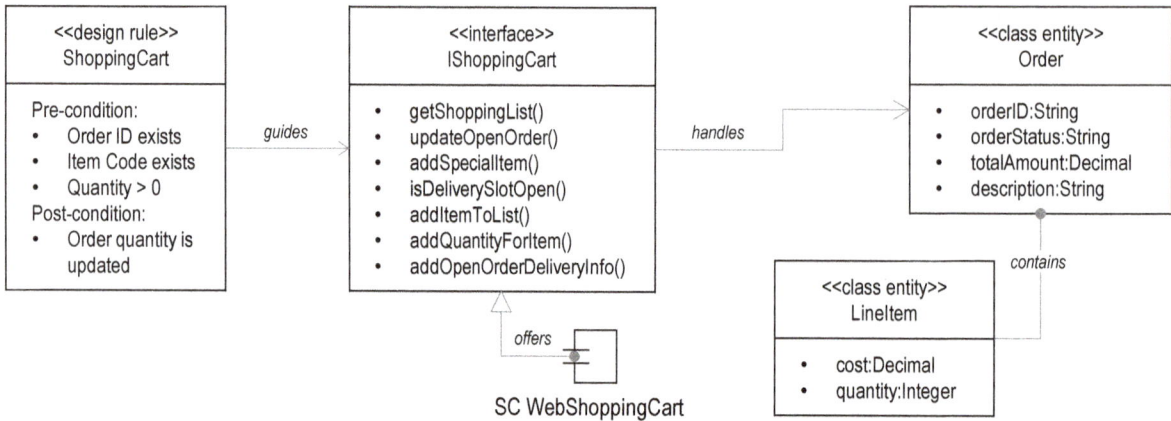

Figure 50: OPS Service Component Interface Responsibility

Please note that the operation signature and return type expression within the interface responsibility, such as fulfillment (order object) : boolean, are routinely specified during the design phase.

## 4.2.4.4.3 Service Component Realization

The OPS project has several programming language choices for the homegrown application programs: C++, C#, Java, Python, Go, Rust, and the like. Figure 51 shows the realization specification in Java, and Figure 52 shows the same in C#.

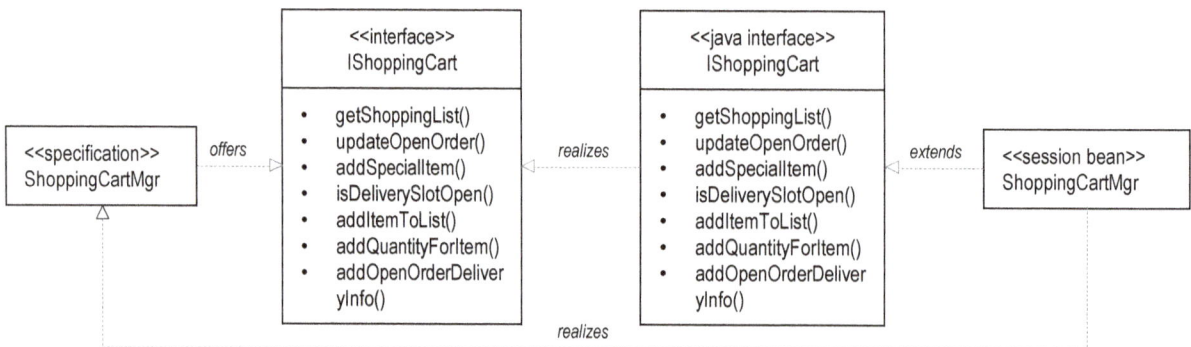

Figure 51: OPS Service Component Realization Specification in Java

Figure 52: OPS Service Component Realization Specification in C#

Aside from the key correlation relationships among the OPS application packages that are seen from the modeling, the architect is likely involved in the implementation package structure definition to ensure all services are well in place and all dependencies including utility resources, bundles (if any), and module dependencies are clarified based on the critical NFR factors.

## 4.2.4.4.4 Service Interface API Specification

Table 42 shows an OPS service API specification through an element property description.

| Element | Property | Description |
|---|---|---|
| SI-3 | Name | Get Details of Order Items |
| | Type | Service Component Interface |
| | Category | API definition |
| | ExposureScope | Public – Restricted Access |
| | APIUsageLevel | Business API |
| | APIOwner | OIM/Eric Owen |
| | url | /v4/orders |
| | Request Method | GET |
| | Response Content Type | application/json |
| | Parameter type | query |
| | Parameter data type | string |
| | Implementation Note | Get order item details for a batch of items |
| | Response Class – Model Schema | {<br>    "orderItems": [ |

| Element | Property | Description |
|---|---|---|
| | | {<br>"quantity": 0,<br>"orderId": "",<br>"orderItemId": "",<br>"price": {<br>  "sellingPrice": 0,<br>  "total": 0,<br>},<br>"hold": false,<br>"subItems": [<br>  "SearchOrderItem"<br>],<br>"sku": "",<br>"orderDate": "DateTime",<br>"stateDocuments": [<br>  ""<br>],<br>"status": "OrderItemState",<br>  }<br> ]<br>} |

Table 42: Service API – Element Property

The service interface plays a critical role throughout this IT service-based model. Through API interfaces, the OPS system exchanges information with other systems, vendors or suppliers, because the ultimate goal of service-orientation is the API economy. The OPS solution builds up an API mediation layer that maps outer APIs to inner APIs and covers the API governance policy, API repository (an overriding capability), API gateway, API management engine, and API developer portal.

# 4.2.5 Infrastructural Area

The infrastructural area primarily handles the OPS solution's SLA concerns. It helps the NFR review and static testing (in the early SDLC[61]). The following shows the OPS

---

[61] SDLC – Software Development Life Cycle

packaging mapping view, the OPS operational deployment view (logical and physical), and the NFR static walkthrough view.

# 4.2.5.1 Package Mapping View

Table 43 exhibits a selected deployment package mapping view property, and Table 44 shows a package element property specification.

Figure 53 mirrors how the various functional services are mapped into the run-time deployment packages and the server environment.

| View | Property | Description |
|---|---|---|
| DPM-1 | Name | OPS Deployment Mapping |
| | Type | Deployment Package Mapping |
| | IsMatrixView | N |

Note:
— The deployment package mapping is a very time-consuming process, requiring lots of architectural thinking, both decisional and structural. The package placement decision is primarily based on the non-functional characteristics of the contained functions services. It has a major impact to the transition from the functional services to the operational runtime performance, as oftentimes the package placement helps restructure some of the functional services for improved service-level characteristics in their packaged environment.

Table 43: Deployment Package Mapping – View Property

| Element | Property | Description |
|---|---|---|
| DP-1 | Name | Web OPS App |
| | Type | Deployment Package |
| | PackageFormat | .jar |
| | InstallationRepository | /repository/order/v3 |
| | TestSpec | Race Condition II |
| | DeliveryStage | Build |

Table 44: Deployment Package Mapping – Element Property

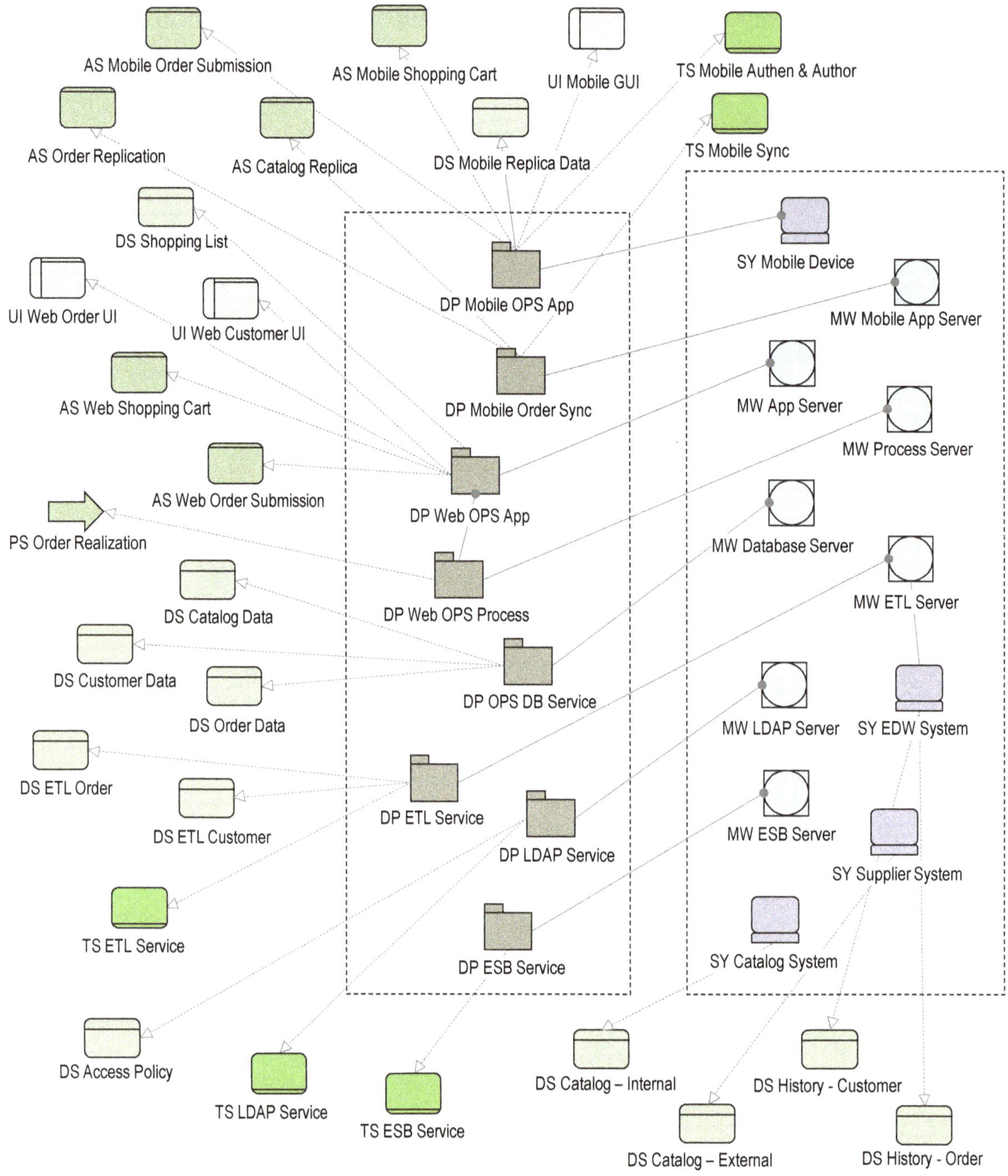

Figure 53: OPS Deployment Package Mapping View

# 4.2.5.2 Deployment View – Logical

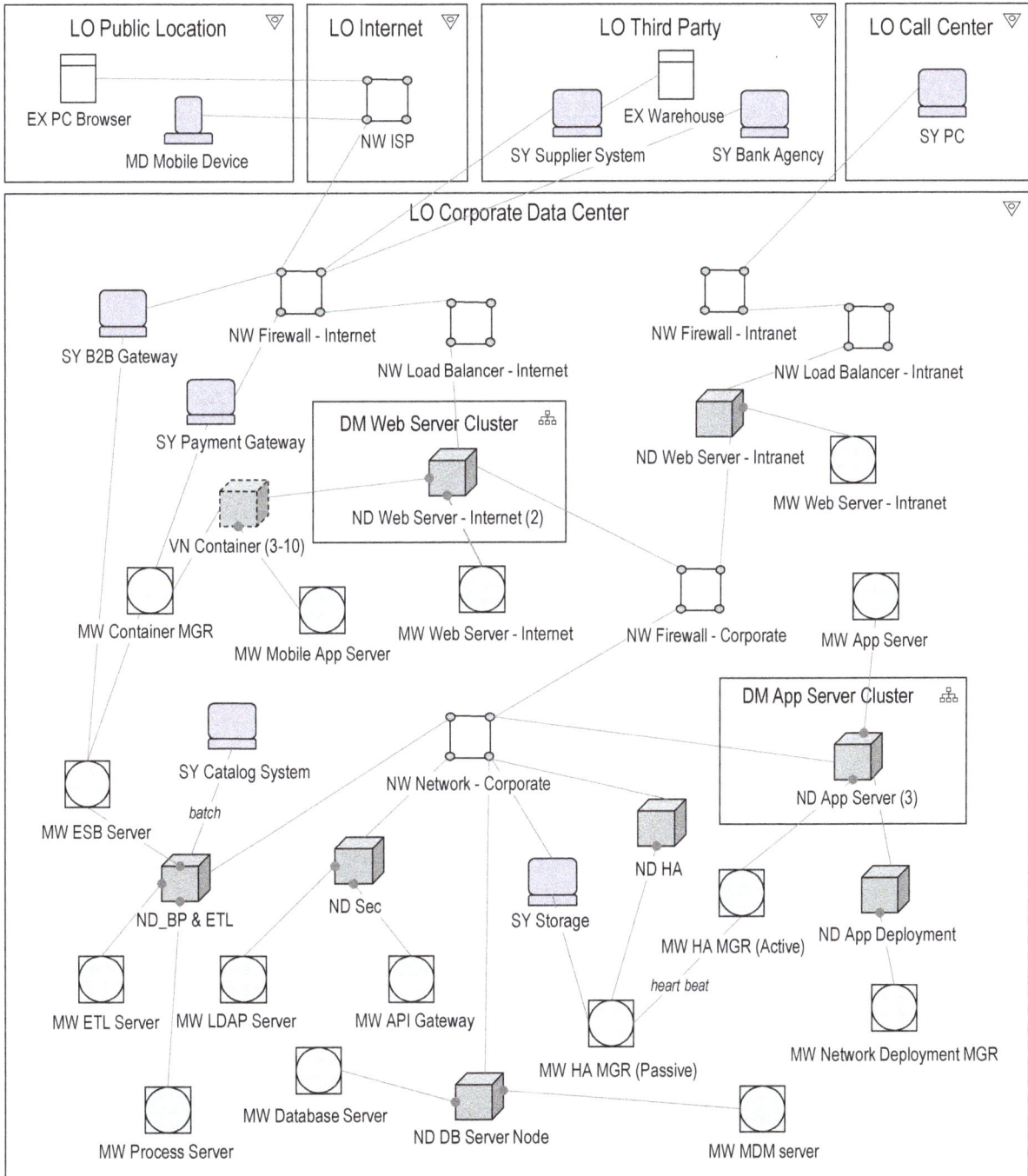

Figure 54: OPS Deployment View

Figure 54 shows the overall deployment view for the OPS solution, and Table 45 specifies some of its element properties.

| Element | Property | Description |
|---------|----------|-------------|
| ND-7 | Name | LDAP Security |
| | IsContainer | No |
| | UtilizationRate | 30% |
| | MTTF-H/W | 100000 hours |
| | MTTF-O/S | 800 hours |
| | MTTR-H/W | 4 hours |
| | MTTR-O/S | 2 hours |
| | ProductID | 9827676XZB-ND884 |
| | Hardware | 2 x Intel Xeon Server |
| | OS | Windows Server 8 |
| | CPUs | CPU E5-2630 0 @ 2.30GHz |
| | RAM | 4G |
| | Manufacturer | Lenovo |
| | Model | X3650 M5 |
| | VM | JBOSS_WinServerR2_26.32.2.16 |
| | Disk | 300G 15K*8/900G 10K*8 |
| | RAID | 10 |
| | DisasterRecovery | Replacement within 12 hours |
| | Backup | MW-124 |
| | SecurityZone | Controlled |
| NW-3 | Name | Firewall – Corporate |
| | Type | Network |
| | Bandwidth-TPS | 200k |
| | IP | 100.10.3.34 |
| | ProductID | 9878359NHB-NW564 |
| | NetworkType | Firewall |
| | Product | Cisco Catalyst 4180 |
| LO-2 | Name | Corporate Data Center |
| | Type | Location |
| | Cardinality | 1 |
| DM-30 | Name | Web Server Cluster |
| | Category | Clustering |
| | SecurityZone | Yellow |

Table 45: Deployment View – Element Property

# 4.2.5.3 Deployment View – Physical

Figure 55 is the physical view of the OPS deployment picture, presented with specific product instances. Table 46 lists some of the view's element properties.

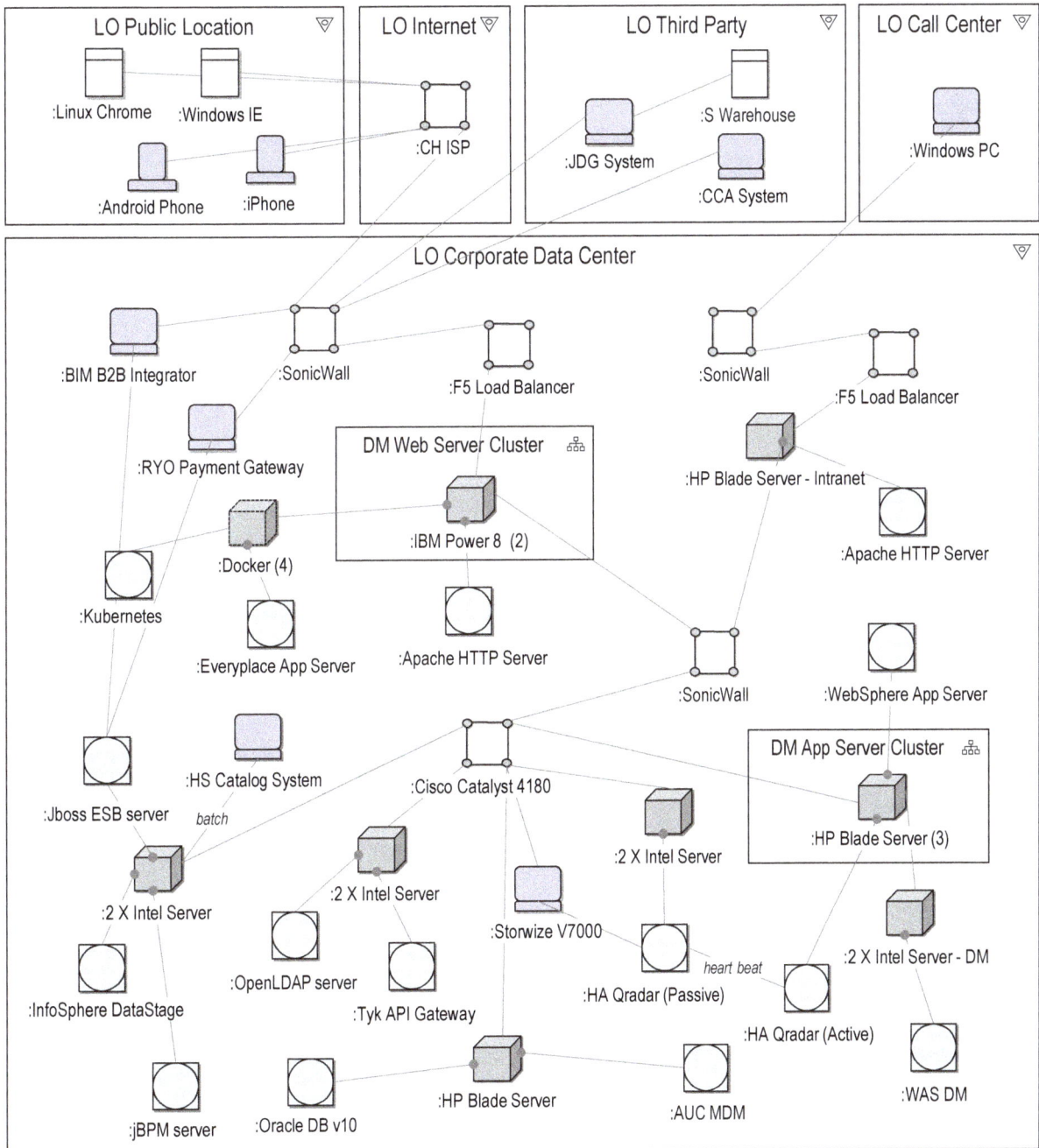

Figure 55: OPS Physical Deployment View

| Element | Property | Description |
|---|---|---|
| MW-17 | Name | ESB Server |
|  | Type | Middleware |
|  | Product | Jboss ESB server |
|  | ProductID | 9878469NUB-MW244 |
| SY-1 | Name | Mobile Device – Wireless |
|  | Type | System |
|  | IsMobileDevice | Y |
|  | IsSensor | N |
| SY-6 | Name | Supplier System |
|  | Product | JDG System |
|  | IsSaaS | N |

Table 46: Physical Deployment View – Element Property

## 4.2.5.4 Deployment View – Throughput Estimation

This section shows a rough estimation of OPS performance throughput based on an initial set of input information relating to order processing (excluding order fulfillment). Figure 56 shows the walkthrough scenario case, and Table 47 presents an estimation process through the property specifications.

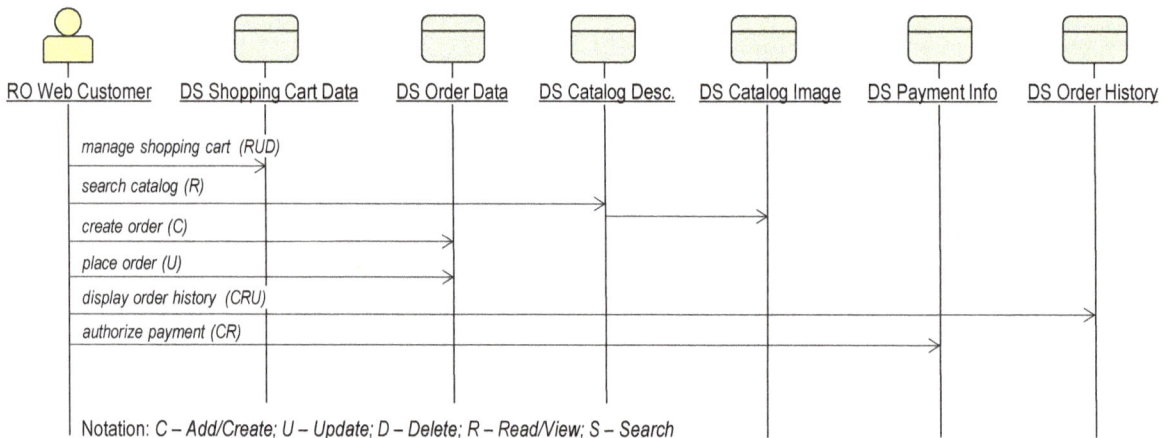

Figure 56: OPS Deployment Walk-thru View – Throughput Estimation

| View | Property | Description |
|---|---|---|
| DEP-3 | Name | OPS Deployment View |
| | Type | Deployment View |
| | IsQuantitativeView | Y |
| | IsThroughputEstimationMode | Y |
| | Transaction/Hour | 1000 |
| | Data Size (kb) | B – Order = 50 |
| | Data Size (kb) | C – Catalog Description = 23 |
| | Data Size (kb) | D – Catalog Image = 150 |
| | Data Size (kb) | E – Shopping List = 10 |
| | Data Size (kb) | A – Order History = 52 |
| | Transaction Mix (frequency/hour*size) | Create Order = 1*E (frequency/hour*size) |
| | Transaction Mix (frequency/hour*size) | Add/Update/Delete Item = 30*B (frequency/hour*size) |
| | Transaction Mix (frequency/hour*size) | Search item by Category = 20*(C+D) (frequency/hour*size) |
| | Transaction Mix (frequency/hour*size) | View Order History = 2*A (frequency/hour*size) |
| | Transaction Mix (frequency/hour*size) | Payment Authorization = 1*B (frequency/hour*size) |
| | Transaction Mix (frequency/hour*size) | Order Placement = 1*B (frequency/hour*size) |
| | TPS Estimation Formula | ((SUM(transaction mix)*transaction per hour)/3600)*8 |
| | Estimated TPS (transaction/s) | 11498 |
| | TPS Scope | Selected Node |

Note:
— The table lists the required properties to calculate the significant portion of throughput (*tps*) as part of predictive scaling (sunny-day scenarios) estimation.
— The estimation result depends on the input credibility – the peak number of requests per second. Inputs also include data concurrency, volatility, and CRUD.
— The TPC[62]-C standard can also be used to calculate tpmC (transactions per minute, type C) and then estimate the corresponding server processing power.
— This is only to illustrate a round of rough estimation. Please use with caution.
— It's suggested to leverage some good online tools, and input the right set of seed data to gain insight into solution stack behavior and bottlenecks in the cloud.

Table 47: Deployment Walk-thru View – Element Property Attributes

---

[62] Transaction Processing Performance Council

# 4.2.5.5 Deployment View – Caching

Figure 57 shows where and how OPS caching is used, one of the NFR concerns in performance and availability.

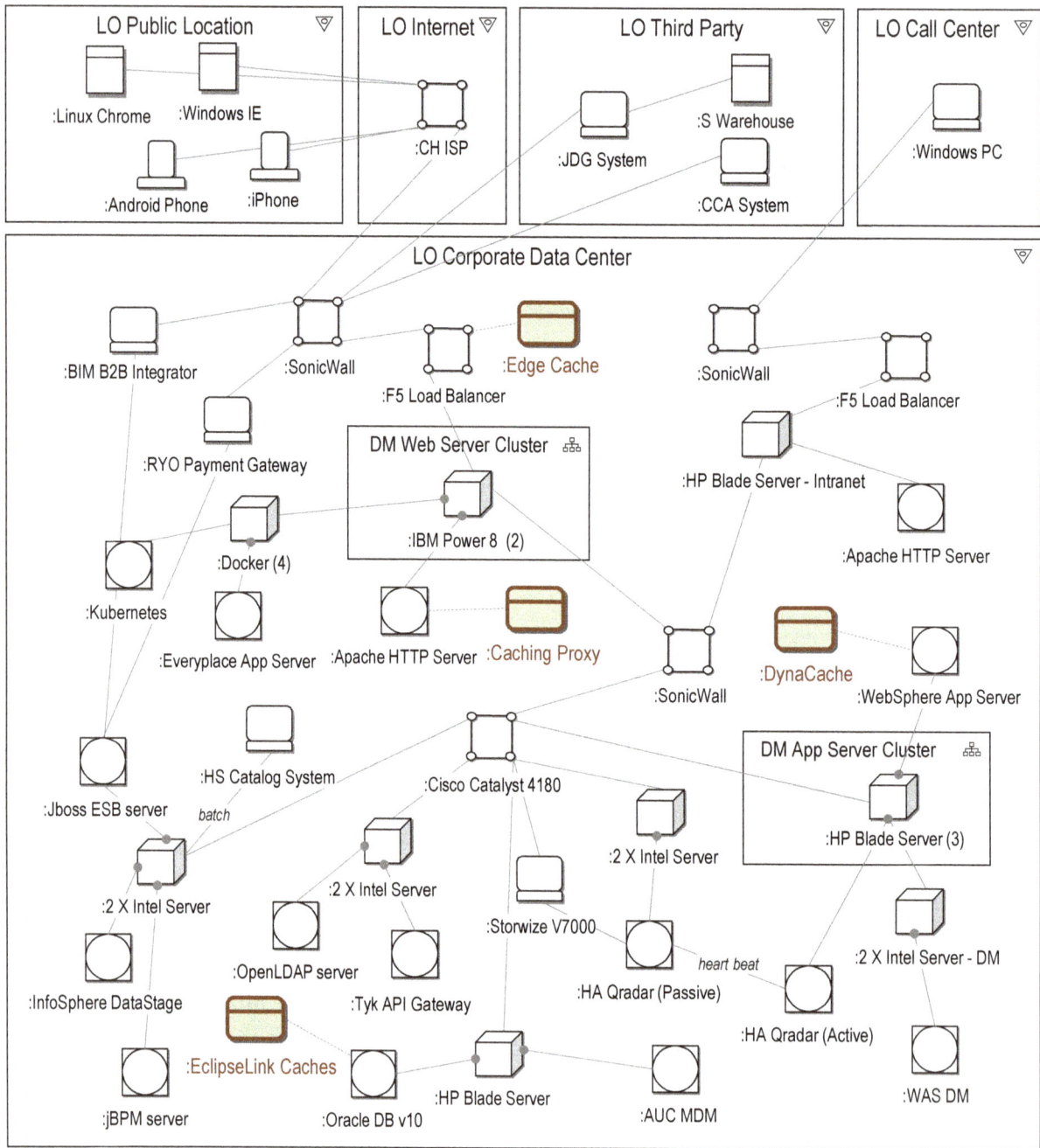

Figure 57: OPS Deployment View – Caching

# 4.2.5.6 Deployment View – Configuration

Figure 58 is a physical configuration view displaying hardware, operating system, and middleware specifications.

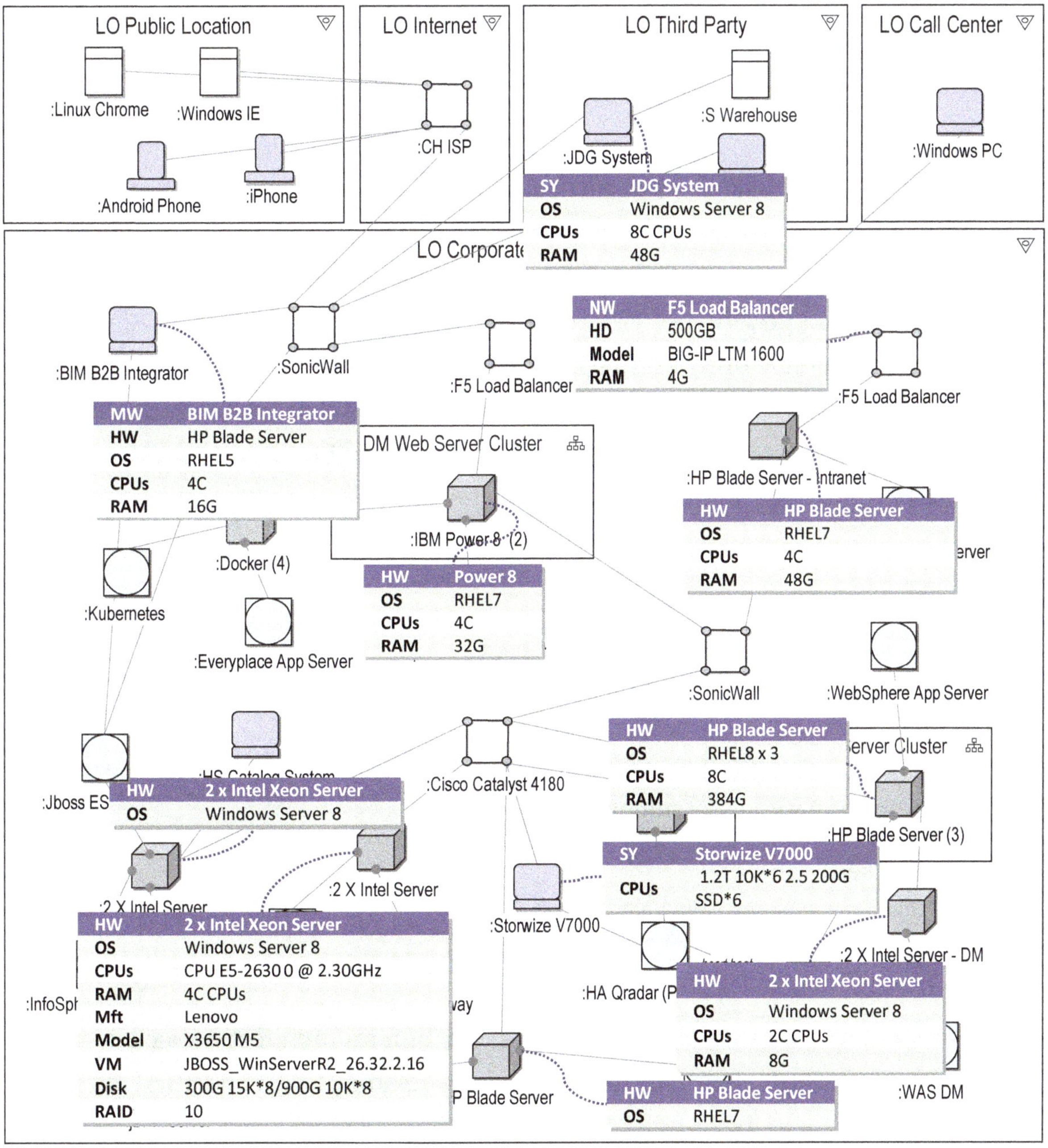

Figure 58: OPS Deployment Configuration View

# Chapter 5  IT Architecture Assessment

IT architecture assessment, a step further in the modeling process, is a process of governance wherein a group of chosen members and AI bots, collectively referred to as the governance body, go through an architectural checklist and give ratings on the basis of the predetermined governance criteria. The criteria are gleaned from EA, standards, assets, reference architectures, leading practices, etc. The governance body determines which activities are supposed to be governed, who reviews and approves decisions, and how escalations occur to ensure the architecture deliverable is imposed by the agile governance or light-weight guardrails.

## 5.1 Assessment Intent and Scope

The following is a comprehensive overview of the situational purpose, scope, and criteria of the governance assessment.

### 5.1.1 Assessment Situation

Why is governance assessment a vital process? A human architect, especially a junior architect may fall short of certain expectations in relation to architectural proficiency even while possessing the requisite modeling tools. An overarching group review ensures architectural replays and third-eye examinations to have the architecture adequately measured and validated. This is particularly true in an agile environment with highly distributed systems and diversified teams. This, in turn, ensures that only an acceptable and reliable architecture model will be in place for each solution release during the design, development, operation, or maintenance.

The following are situations when an assessment is necessitated:
— As a periodic review of an existing architecture solution
— New project or new requirement enhancement
— Migration needs
— Architect qualification reviews
— New standard or compliance requirement
— Identified risk items

# 5.1.1.1 Validation vs. Assessment in the Context

A validated solution project without undergoing a detailed assessment may fail, because a solution validation alone does not warrant architectural viability beyond a single-solution scope.

Traditionally, the IT architectural validation process covers validation of requirements, unit test, integration test, systems test, systems integration test, acceptance test, performance test, regression tests, etc. For an exhaustive validation, an architect needs to have validation planning and test specification in place.

Here, the architecture assessment from a governance perspective primarily plays up the valuable static testing that entails prototyping, mock-up, walkthrough inspection, paper testing, modeling mapping, evaluation or fitness function design, project replay, and estimated simulations, in conformance to various enterprise and industry standards.

In addition, the governance assessment process involves an expert group evaluation, led by SME and directed by reference architecture (RA), leading practices, guidelines, etc. In fact, one of the key skills of an architecture practitioner is the ability to use the asset or leading practice to prevent reinventing the wheel.

For each enterprise solution, there are usually several assessment cases, exemplified in the following:

— If a Java framework is needed for developing ops-friendly, high-performance, and RESTful web services, Dropwizard would be an architectural option.
— If adopting a BDD,[63] Gherkin DSL[64] would be the choice.
— If using a Circuit Breaker pattern, Netflix's Hystrix library would provide an open-source framework solution that deals with issues like latency and fault-tolerance in the complex and distributed systems.
— If aiming for a better QPS[65] than Nginx, Taobao's Tengine middleware would embed a load-balance algorithm for HA and performance.

Put simply, the difference between the solution modeling validation and governance assessment is that the former is for *assurance of customer requirements* while the latter is principally for *architectural conformance*. As a caveat, the terminology difference is anticipated to become more inconsequential, as validation and guidance assessment are now becoming more intertwined, especially in an AI-powered system environment.

# 5.1.1.2 Assessment for Agile Governance

In an agile architecture culture, an organization is largely composed of self-governing teams without much portfolio management. In contrast to the traditional architecture governance model that becomes disconnected from solution architecture, the agile architecture assessment requires a readily applicable governance framework closely attached to solution architecture, possibly through an automated assessment mechanism.

For an agile architecture, governance review is a constant process, and is applicable to both green-field and brown-field solution approaches. It's recommended for migration or transitional architecture to establish views regarding the current state as well as target state for gap assessment. In straightforward terms, agile in scale without architectural governance is most assuredly fragile.

---

[63] Behavior-Driven Development
[64] Domain Specific Language
[65] Queries Per Second

# 5.1.2 Assessment Scope

Though the architecture governance includes principle, compliance, risk, etc., and encompasses an extensive scope, this book is primarily concerned with the IT architecture governance and not the IT management. The latter is typically envisaged as a task restricted to resource allocation and smooth operations. As evident in this book, the term *IT services* in solution architecture governance deviates semantically from the IT services in operational runtime maintenance management.

The examples of the IT architecture governance in this book are intentionally limited to modeling enhancement.

# 5.1.3 Assessment Criteria

Governance assessment criteria come from diverse sources, primarily from the governance standard or framework, each applicable in a specific situation. For instance, COBIT[66] differs from other frameworks by focusing on security, risk management, and information governance; DPIA[67] under the GDPR[68] targets data protection in designated regions. Please note that this book zeroes in on the solution architecture governance, rather than the operational maintenance governance, therefore, most IT service standards are only partially referenced.

IT governance includes both a governance body and governance procedures specified in the predefined standards (industry, IT, or corporate enterprise). For example, information governance from an IT standard encompasses the following:
— Executive Sponsors and Champions
— Organizational Structure and Definitions of Roles and Responsibilities
— Information Governance Experts
— Data Stewards, Data Managers

---

[66] Control Objectives for Information and related Technology
[67] Data Protection Impact Assessment
[68] General Data Protection Regulation

— Data Quality Experts
— Data Standardization Processes
— Processes and Business Rules for ongoing Governance
— Information Governance Policies and Procedures
— Common Data Standards and Business Definitions
— Data Quality Remediation Processes
— Change Management Processes (IT & Business)
— Repositories, populated with the Common Data Standards,
— Business Definitions, Data Structures, and Data Transformation Rules
— Workflow Technology
— Data Quality Remediation Technology
— Integrated Development and Information Management Platform
— Reporting & Performance Management Technology

The standard specifications can be incorporated into the models in a simplified and abstract fashion. Additionally, the criteria can glean from the following macro- and micro-level guidance for the solution architecture governance.

The *macro-level guidance* on solution realization customarily includes:
— Helping specify the *design principles* that can be part of architecture principles and ensuring they are applied consistently.
— Assisting in *user experience design*, preferably with GUI mockup tools.
— For homegrown applications, helping set up the *development environment* and map *application or development framework*, etc., defined from architecture metrics or patterns, and decide the programming language(s) to be used, and illustrate code mapping if needed.
— Assisting with the *structure of application modules.*
— Reaching agreement with the designers or developers prior to implementation, and establishing *traceability* from architecture views to design diagrams and documents associated with view or element's property (realization, source repository or attachment).
— Defining the test plan and specifying the *initial test specifications* (test cases can also be created via the model).
— Determining *component realization mechanism* (in-house custom development, outsourcing, integration, configuration, transformation, cloud subscription, purchase of ready-made solution, bespoke web or mobile application package, ERP customization, etc.).

The *micro-level guidance* is more toward the solution design beyond the ESA scope, such as detailed component design, design pattern, data design, detailed test specifications, or network design. These are the better-to-have items. It's up to individual architects under a certain circumstance to delve more into the lower-level design as a proof of architecture. When needed, architects can include those detailed design requirements as part of relevant architecture property attributes.

This book does not delineate the attribute criteria for the assessment. For attribute-guided solution architecture assessment, a set of common methods can be referenced, such as ATAM,[69] CBAM,[70] scenario-based SAAM,[71] and QFD[72] mapping.

# 5.2 An Assessment Walkthrough

The following is an example of an architecture assessment as a part of IT governance. A simple *checklist approach* is used, and it is followed by an iterative modeling enhancement. It is anticipated that mapping enterprise governance metrics with solution views and elements will help close gaps that are frequently observable in the traditional architectural review process.

## 5.2.1 Architectural Checklist

Even with guiding principles and an individual architect's seasoned expertise in a solution environment, things can still slip through the cracks. From the viewpoint of an enterprise as a whole, governance must be in place to ensure the solution's architecture conformance. The following is a checklist (Table 48) for the OPS project exemplified in Chapter 4.

---

[69] Architecture Trade-off Analysis Method
[70] Cost-Benefit Analysis Method
[71] Software Architecture Analysis Method
[72] Quality Functional Deployment

| Category | Checklist | Rate | Relevance |
|----------|-----------|------|-----------|
| Architecture Overview | Is the boundary clearly defined? | A | — AO |
| | What's the architectural style, patterns, or reference architecture? | A | — IT service-based architecture <br> — Pattern |
| | | I | — Reference architecture |
| | Is a clear roadmap planned? A capability framework already in place? | A | — Capability |
| Functional Service | Is the functional definition clear? How are the requirement verification and mapping? | A | — Case scenario <br> — Service interaction view |
| | Is the functional interface justifiable? How is reusability? | A | — Service component interface specification <br> — Programming code reuse |
| | | A | — Proven application framework (Spring Boot) |
| | Is the module design rationale? What's the rationale for granularity? | A | — Domain definition <br> — Composite service identification <br> — Core service specification |
| | How is the completeness of functional service definition (layering, abstraction, isolation, and interoperability)? | A | — Functional service modeling <br> — Rule specification |
| | | A | — Service abstraction |
| | | A | — Service invocation separate from implementation details |
| | | A | — Non-core application service dependent on core application service |
| | Do all the functional requirements map key NFRs? | A | — Deployment package mapping |
| | | A | — Horizontal scaling pattern |
| | | A | — Modular services for stability <br> — IT service-based reuse |
| Data Service | Is data domain, data service, or data relationship clear? | A | — Data service loosely coupled with data item <br> — Data service abstraction |
| | | A | — Data service validation |
| | Do data integration and callback conform to the standard? | I | — Specific rules and metrics including timeout limit for sync invocation |
| | | A | — Asynchronous ESB callback |
| | Are data source and data consumption clear? | A | — Separate read and write data <br> — Separate hot and cold data |

| Category | Checklist | Rate | Relevance |
|---|---|---|---|
| | | I | — Mapping approach between data service and data item or data entity, as a guidance |
| | | I | — Database or data table partitioning<br>— Optional auto sharding or data sharding |
| | Does the data access conform to standard specifications such as LDAP, ESB, and MDM? | A | — DB only accessible via data service interface |
| | | A | — Middleware specifications |
| | | A | — Unified metadata and master data management (MDM) |
| | Are data quality and control already in place? | A | — Critical data in active and standby mode |
| | | A | — Data quality middleware |
| | Is data federation or distribution clear? | A | — Data invocation across business domain (ESB) |
| | | A | — Federated data service (federation middleware) |
| | | A | — Asynchronous communication for non- real-time business (order fulfillment)<br>— Idempotency scenarios |
| | How is data transactional integrity? | I | — Double write consistency between distributed caching and database (leading practice) |
| | | I | — Distributed transaction framework |
| Platform/ Operation | Is the development platform well defined (java generic development platform, or mobile app development platform)? | A | — Allowing automated software version rollback (DevOps) |
| | | A | — Blue/green deployment for web platform (DevOps) |
| | | A | — Rolling deployment for mobile platform (DevOps) |
| | Is it satisfied with the infrastructure environment (standardization, specification, reliability compatibility, and expandability) for the distributed architecture? | A | — Reusable NFR services and middleware |
| | | A | — Automatic runtime service governance |
| | | P | — Degradable runtime service<br>— Concurrency control |

| Category | Checklist | Rate | Relevance |
|---|---|---|---|
| | | P | — Fault-tolerance<br>— Circuit-breaker<br>— Server whitelist |
| | | I | — Distributed tracing and monitoring |
| | How is the overall performance and availability consideration? | I | — Availability estimation |
| | How is the capacity or resource utilization? | A | — Use of cache and cache invalidation |
| | | I | — 4 times of required service capacity<br>— 2 times of deployment capacity |
| | Is the node interface connection evaluated? | A | — Deployment view |
| | Is the key system configuration info complete or accurate? | A | — Deployment configuration view |
| | Is RTO/RPO analyzed? How is the disaster recovery plan? | I | — Redundant data center DR capacity |
| Security | How is authentication and authorization considered? | A | — Security middleware |
| | Is confidentiality or sensitive data transmission well-controlled? | I | — Deployment security view |
| | Is application security assured? Is any strong measure against web attack? | I | — Intrusion prevention (IPS) middleware |
| | | A | — Deployment walk-thru |
| | | A | — Reliable firewall |
| | | A | — DDoS |

Note:
— For simplicity, rating criteria: Accepted (A), Improve (I), Pending (P)
— Each of the architectural considerations in the table can be further broken down. For example, degradable runtime service and concurrency control for HA can take more analytical steps.
— The checklist may include other consideration criteria such as priority, reviewer, and action deadline.

Table 48: Architectural Checklist for OPS Solution

The architecture assessment can take various forms. It can serve as an index list to the architecture model, cross-checking the validity and viability of the dynamic structure and decisions made therein.

# 5.2.2 Model Enhancement

This section shows the OPS model enhancement, following the action items specified in the earlier architectural checklist.

Based on the extensive architectural review, the required enhancements (Table 49) include addition or revision of the former OPS solution architecture.

| Governance Item | Action | N/M | Visual View |
|---|---|---|---|
| Reference architecture for API management | Create an API management reference architecture | N | API management RA (Figure 60) |
| Timeout for application server domain | Add Rule: DISTRIBUTED_LOCK_TIMEOUT > JTA Timeout & Stuck Thread Timeout > JTA Timeout | N | N/A |
| Mapping approach between data service and data entity | Map service component with its corresponding entities | N | Service component realization: entity – class diagram (Figure 61) |
| Database partitioning technique | Choose a proper pattern | N | Pattern – data sharding |
| Double write consistency between caching and database | Adopt the leading practice from the AGC implementation | N | To-Do |
| Distributed transaction framework | Follow TCC[73] mechanism | N | Pattern – TCC (Figure 62) |
| Tracing and Monitoring | Create a distributed tracing chart | N | Distributed tracing (Figure 63) |
| Availability estimation | Estimate high availability (HA) based on the current info | M | Deployment – high availability estimation (Figure 64) |
| Capacity planning | Add architectural key choices:<br>— 4 times required IT service capacity<br>— 2 times required deployment capacity | N | N/A |
| Disaster recovery plan | Create an initial disaster recovery plan | N | DR plan (Figure 65) |
| Data transmission | Go through deployment views and | M | Deployment – security |

[73] TCC (Try-Commit/Confirm-Cancel) transaction

| Governance Item | Action | N/M | Visual View |
|---|---|---|---|
| security | add transmission security considerations | | (Figure 66) |
| Intrusion prevention | Purchase middleware IPS and incorporate it into the deployment view | N | N/A |
| Note:<br>— N/M connotation: New/Modified | | | |

Table 49: List of Architectural Enhancements

Figure 59 is a visual metrics view for actions in Table 49. Table 50 shows the property attributes description of a governance element.

| Element | Property | Description |
|---|---|---|
| GV-1 | Name | Reference Architecture for API Management |
| | Type | Governance |
| | Category | Reference Architecture |
| | Statement | API management needs to follow well-accepted reference architecture or leading practices. |
| | GoverningLayer | DevOps |
| | GoverningLayer | Functional |
| | GoverningStandard | A-ESA |
| | RatingCriteria | HWR Governance Review Criteria.doc |
| | LeadExaminer | Jack Luwinski |
| | ReviewHistory | See "Review Log" |

Table 50: Metrics View (Governance Review) – Element Property

Next, the governance review results are to be incorporated into the existing solution architecture model as specified in Chapter 4. The newly created or modified architecture views are shown in the following sections.

As there are several rounds of processes for governance review and model enhancement, the work-in-progress architecture views have different levels of architectural conformance and assurance in an agile enterprise solution architecture approach.

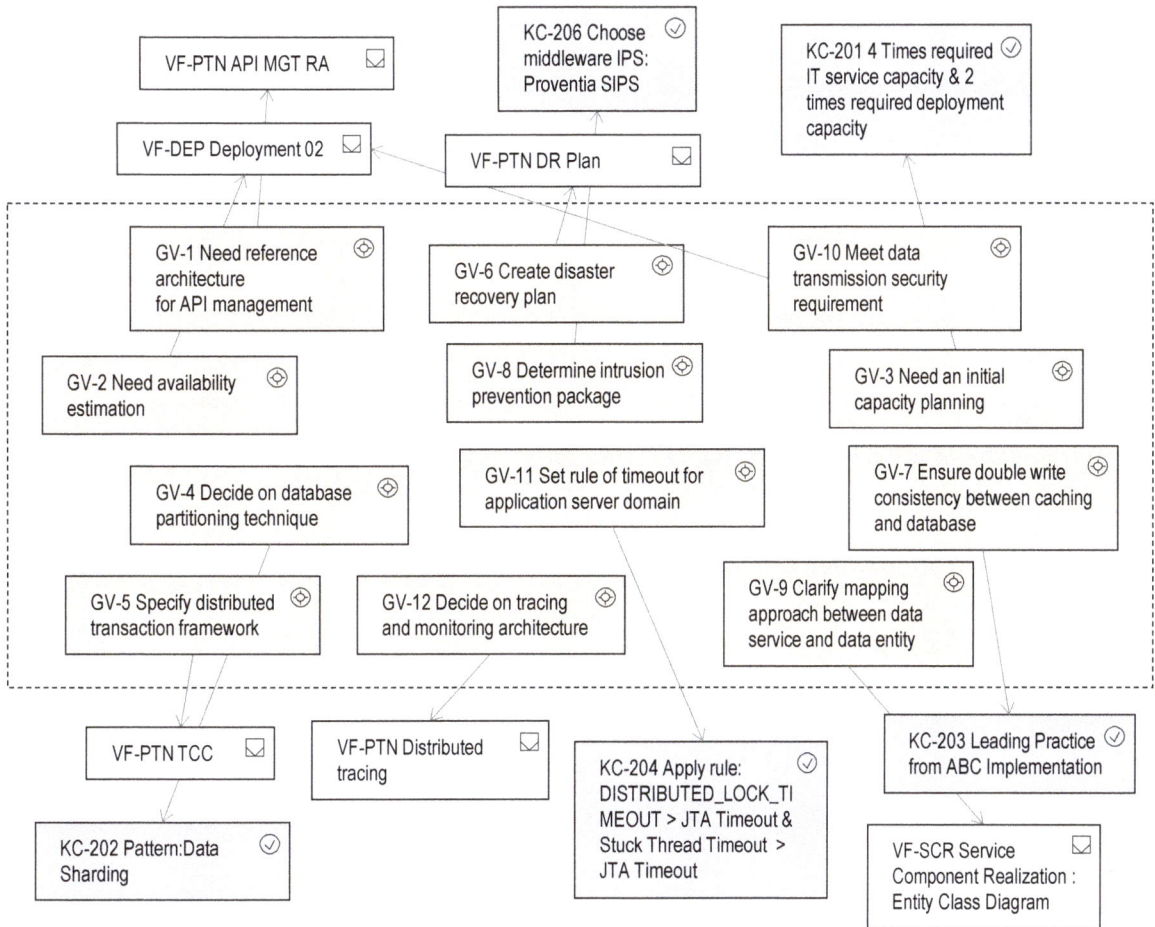

Figure 59: Metrics View (Governance Review)

## 5.2.2.1 Pattern View – API Management RA

Figure 60 is a newly created pattern view for the API management reference architecture.

The RA specifies required API middleware operational environment, including the API gateway, API management engine, API transformation, API analytics, API toolkit and API developer portal.

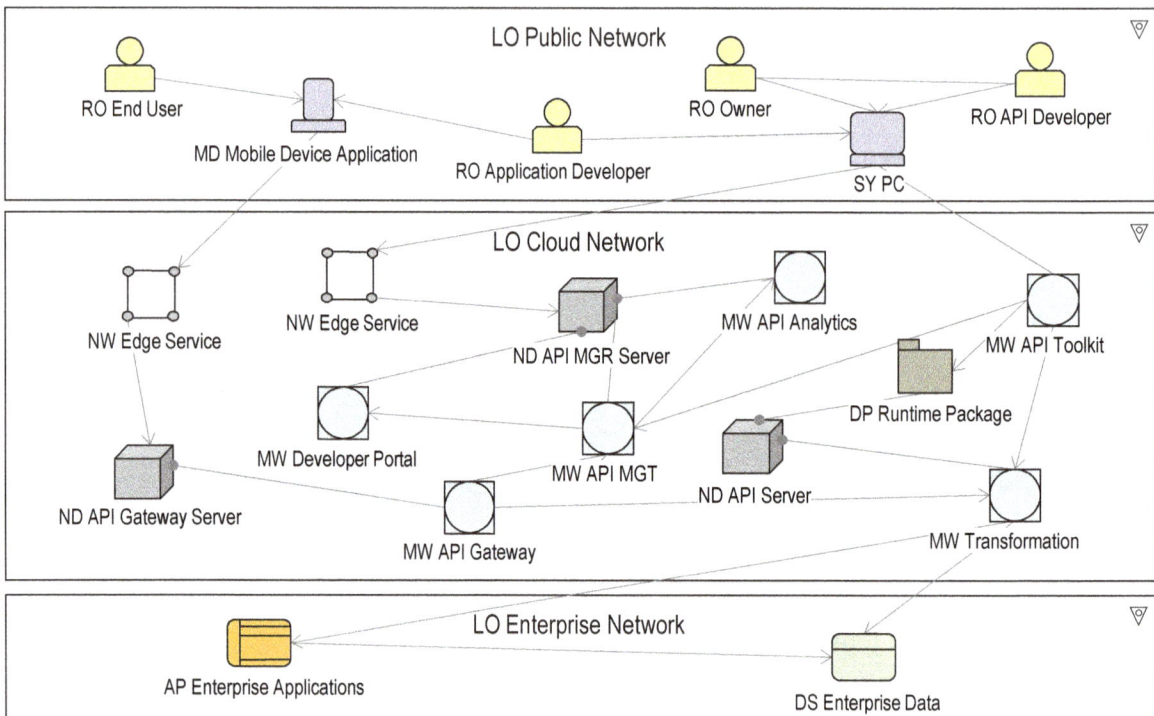

Figure 60: API Management Reference Architecture View

## 5.2.2.2 Service Component Realization – Entity

Figure 61 shows the entity class diagram as guidance for the design specification.

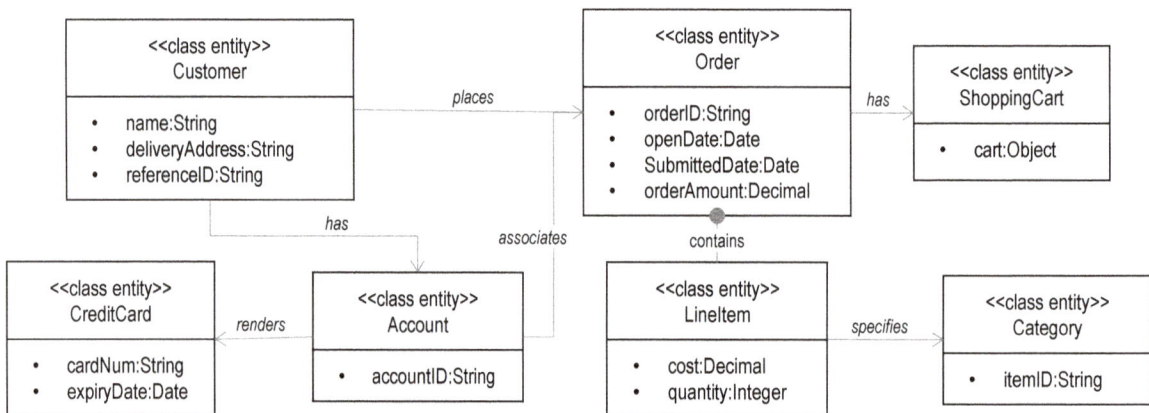

Figure 61: Entity Class Diagram

# 5.2.2.3 Pattern View – TCC Distributed Transaction

Figure 62 is a distributed transaction view, showing a TCC pattern view, based on the requirement rule: to process the account and bonus point in a single transaction.

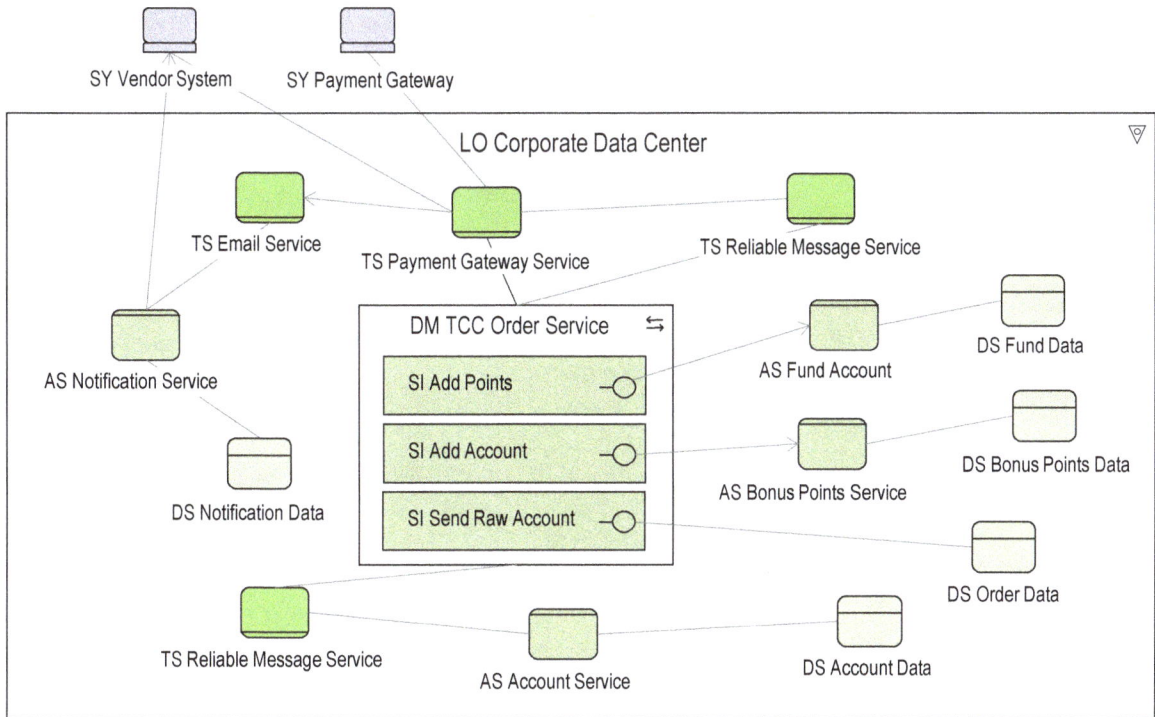

Figure 62: Distributed Transaction View

# 5.2.2.4 Pattern View – Distributed Tracing

Figure 63 is an add-on distributed tracing pattern view.

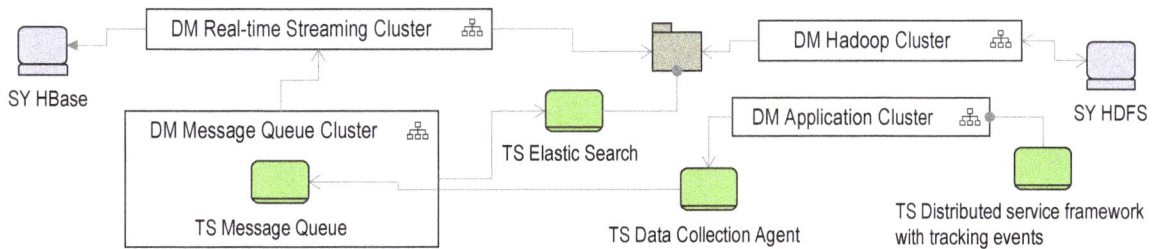

Figure 63: Distributed Tracing Pattern View

# 5.2.2.5 Deployment View – HA Estimation

Figure 64 and Table 51 demonstrate an HA estimation using a static testing approach.

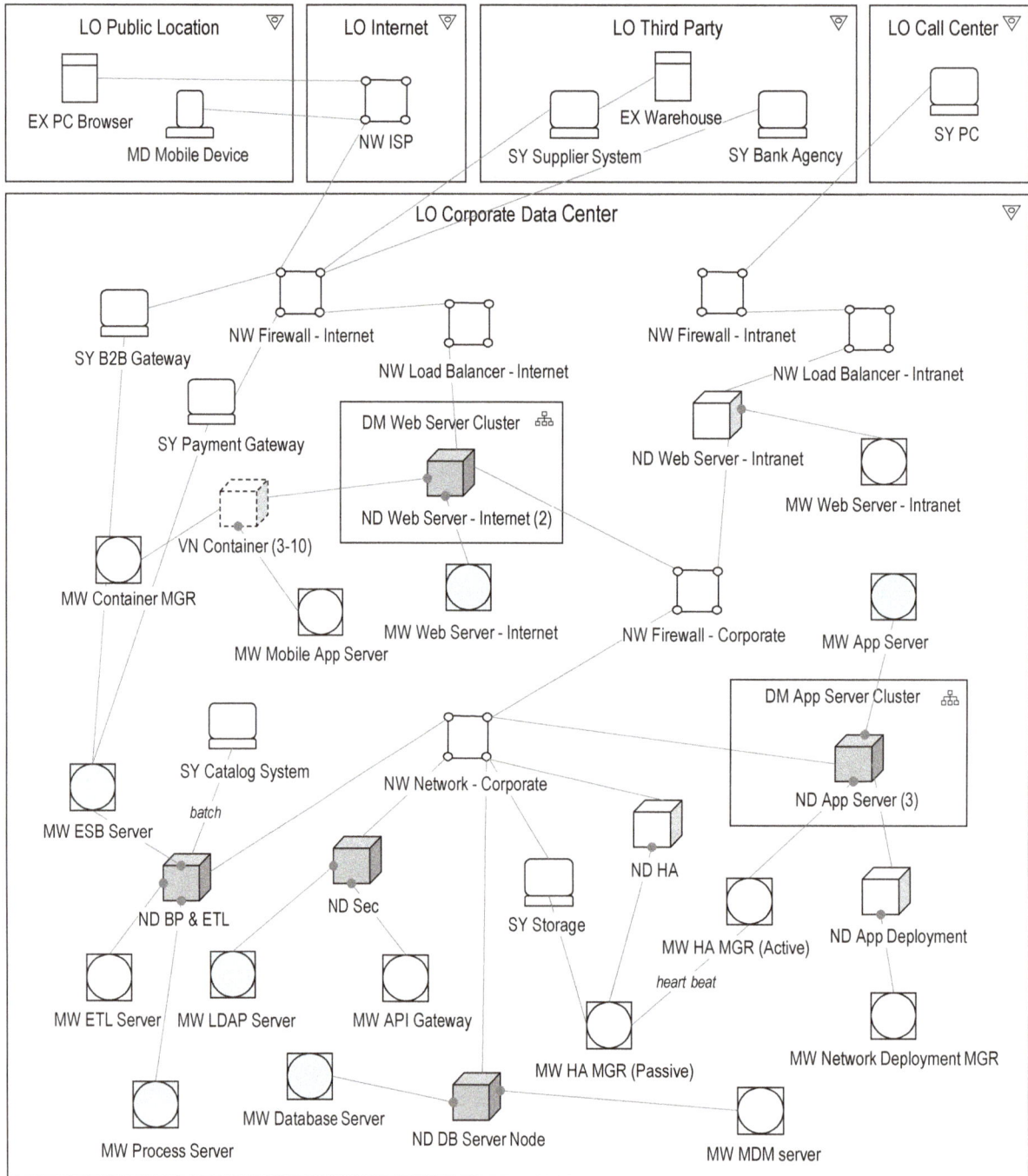

Figure 64: Deployment View – HA Estimation

| View | Property | Description |
|------|----------|-------------|
| DEP-6 | Name | OPS Deployment View |
| | Type | Deployment View |
| | IsAvailabilityEstimationMode | Y |
| | AvailabilityFormula | MTTF/(MTTF+MTTR) |
| | MTTF-Apps(hours) | 300 |
| | MTTF-H/W(hours) | 100000 |
| | MTTF-O/S(hours) | 800 |
| | MTTR-Apps(hours) | 2 |
| | MTTR-H/W(hours) | 4 |
| | MTTR-O/S(hours) | 2 |
| | Availability-Apps | 0.99337748 |
| | Availability-H/W | 0.99996 |
| | Availability-O/S | 0.99750623 |
| | Availability-Node | Web servers = 1 |
| | Availability-Node | App servers = 0.999999 |
| | Availability-Node | LDAP server = 0.997466 |
| | Availability-Node | ESB&BPM servers = 0.990861 |
| | Availability-Node | DB server = 0.990861 |
| | OverallAvailabilityEstimation | 0.97931681 |

Note:
— This is a simplified calculation. Functional service reliability in any node, for example, is treated the same and only the highlighted nodes are counted.
— Availability-Node includes Availability-H/W (hardware), Availability-O/S (operating system), and Availability-Apps (functional services) if any.
— Example calculation process:
   — app server availability=A-H/W*A-O/S*A-App=0.990860598
   — total app service availability = 1- $(1-0.990860598)^3$=0.999999
— In an agile architecture's fail-fast approach, HA emphasis shifts from Mean Time Between Failure (MTBF) to Mean Time to Recovery (MTTR), potentially with intent-based networking. Windowed user-uptime is a way of calculation for meaningful availability.

Table 51: HA Estimation – View Property

# 5.2.2.6 Deployment View – Disaster Recovery

Figure 65 and Table 52 illustrate a disaster recovery plan view and some of its property attributes, as per the governance review process.

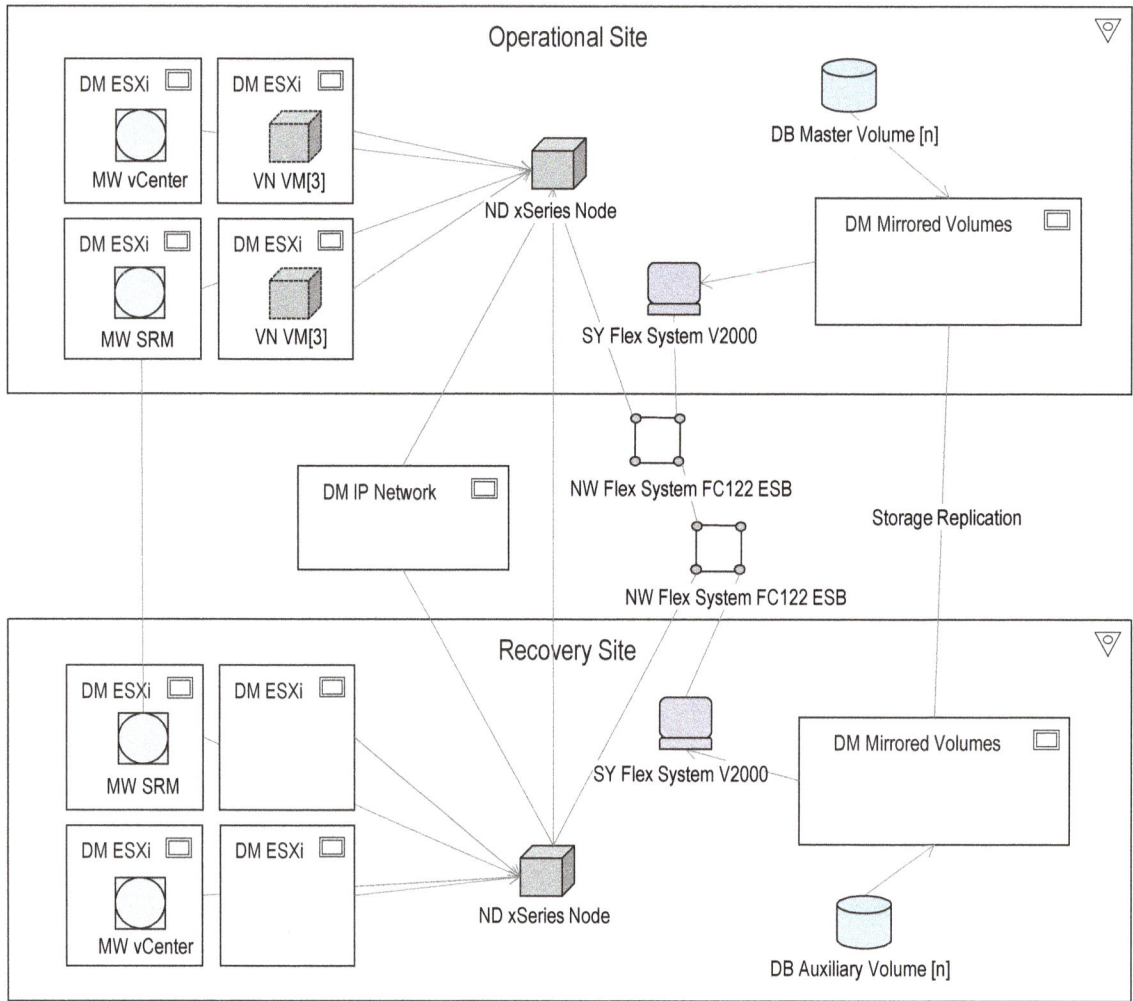

Figure 65: Disaster Recovery Plan View

| Element | Property | Description |
|---------|----------|-------------|
| MW-301 | Name | Site Recovery Manager |
|  | ShortName | SRM |
| NW-303 | SyncMechanism | Async |
|  | Name | Storage Replication |
| LO-32 | Name | Recovery Site |
|  | RTO | 1-4 hours |
|  | RPO | 5-10 minutes |
|  | Cold Standby | 0.2 x Server RU[74] |

Table 52: Disaster Recovery – Element Property Attributes

[74] Resource Units

# 5.2.2.7 Deployment View – Security

Figure 66 is a deployment view with add-on security highlights (zones and protocols).

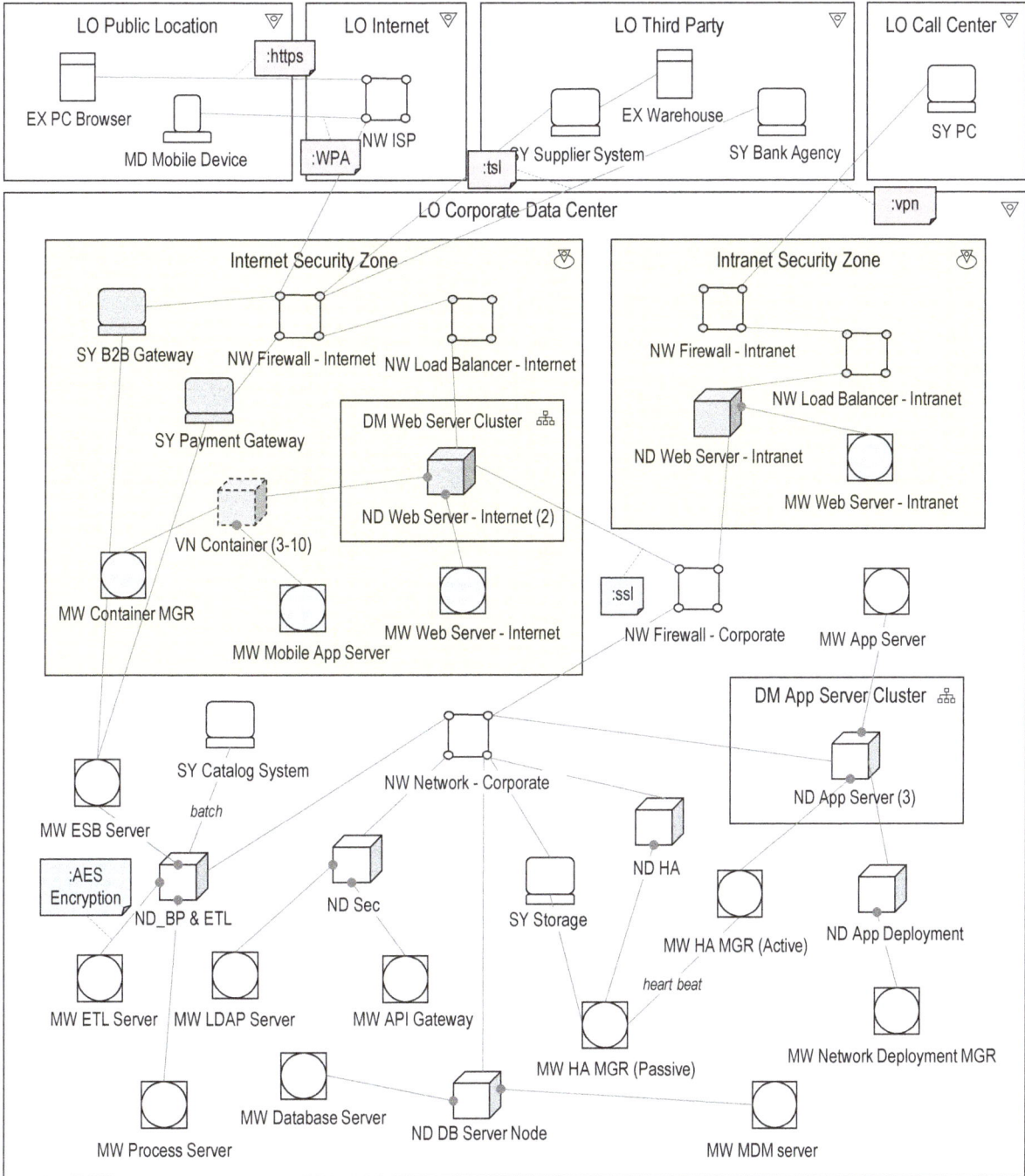

Figure 66: Deployment View (Security)

# 5.2.3 Further Enhancement Work

The preceding figures are either added or modified, based on the governance assessment from two schools of thought: structural and decisional. It can be observed that many improvements (or stepwise refinements) are made from the earlier solution architecture. Therefore, as part of architectural governance, the architecture assessment plays an influential role in architectural quality.

As a step forward, a simulation test can follow up with a tooling and risk analyzer. It should be mentioned that the simulator and modeling tools, when combined with AI, can validate and assess sufficiently, especially for structural validation covering *design time*, *runtime*, and *change time* governance. However, there is no such thing as a fully automated governance process. Decisional architecture still behooves the modeling architects and governance body to ensure sound solution architecture through the review process. Accumulatively, the snapshot review records will result in leading practices for future references.

It's worth noting that the walkthrough mentioned above demonstrates a simplistic architectural assessment process. However, the quality of architecture relies on all sorts of factors, including dependable inputs (aware of GIGO[75]) as well as a strong support team and platform environment. The landing effect is up to requirement management, development process, implementation specification, testing plan, and peer review. Though the abstracted A-ESA model can hardly be a "true reality," it's absolutely instrumental, both structural and decisional, in shaping and governing real enterprise solutions for system robustness and business benefits. Eventually, IT service-based architectural judgment is up to the measurement criteria, including the key IT service stability (other than availability and reliability), service reusability, service capacity, and architectural flexibility and user acceptance levels.

---

[75] Garbage In, Garbage Out.

# Epilogue

This book introduced a modeling approach in a simple yet pragmatic manner. The A-ESA originates from a great deal of practical project experience and the modeling framework applies to most architectural styles: component-based monolithic application, enterprise integration architecture, internally service-oriented application, or distributed service architecture. It allows for flexibility and customization in order to fit diverse architectural needs, be it an enterprise-level product or a platform solution.

It goes without saying that the nuances of the multifarious definitions in this book are subject to debate. However, architectural dogma or pedantic narration is not this book's intent, as it focuses more on reflecting the standpoints from a variety of enterprise-level solution architecture practitioners.

Certain readers may prefer an additional fully fledged presentation with real-world architectural designs, especially the NFR modeling. But, the approach delineated in this book is intended as more of an architectural solution blueprint than a design model.

Bear in mind: *the viability of an enterprise solution architecture isn't decided merely on an enterprise architecture or a solution design; it's determined in an agile architecture model that embraces both of the worlds that matter.*

When envisioning the future, computing processors, chips and systems will be much faster and more compact. IT or DT[76] will be even more service-oriented, automated, and intelligent, and systems will be all the more dynamically configurable, eventually achieving the dream of an *autonomous* enterprise with a complex mesh of brainy

---

[76] Digital Technology

analytical bots, a composable, low-code platform, and governance contrivance. Will IT architecture still have a role to play by then? It does, inevitably, but at a different level and with a different concentration. With more building blocks available, plus platform as a service, IT service-based architecture will be the way out and become more standardized as IT *utility* services.

I hope this book can contribute better ideas to the world of enterprise solution architecture. I can be reached at guc888@gmail.com for comments, criticism, and tooling support.

# Appendix I  Text Conventions

There are two simple text conventions used throughout this book.

1.  *italic* with lower case: Indicates an emphasis. Here is an example: "Keep in mind: *the value of modeling extends way beyond simple visualization*."
2.  *Italic* with upper case: Indicates a special term defined in the A-ESA model. Here is an example: "The *Deployment Package Mapping View* maps each functional service into a runtime package by considering its unique characteristics."

# Appendix II  View Abbreviation

The following is a list of view abbreviations employed in the A-ESA model for ready reference.

| # | Area | View | Abbr. |
|---|------|------|-------|
| 1 | Architecture Overview | Architecture Overview | AOV |
| 2 | Enterprise | Capability | CAP |
| 3 | Infrastructure | Deployment | DEP |
| 4 | Architecture Overview | DevOps | DEV |
| 5 | Architecture Overview | Metrics | MTS |
| 6 | Enterprise | Organization | ORG |
| 7 | Infrastructure | Package Mapping | DPM |
| 8 | Case Scenario | Page Flow | PFV |
| 9 | Architecture Overview | Pattern | PTN |
| 10 | Case Scenario | Process Model | PRM |
| 11 | Architecture Overview | Relationship Validation | VLD |
| 12 | Functional Service | Service Component Realization | SCR |
| 13 | Functional Service | Service Interaction | SIV |
| 14 | Functional Service | Service Relationship | SRV |
| 15 | Case Scenario | Use Case Model | UCM |

# Appendix III  Element List

The following is an element list defined in the A-ESA model. For quicker adoption of this modeling approach, prevailing element definitions and icons from other enterprise architecture specifications and tooling are borrowed as many as possible.

| Area/Category | Element Name | Abbr | Icon | Preferred Display |
|---|---|---|---|---|
| Enterprise | Capability | CP | | |
| Case Scenario | Role | RO | | |
| | Task | TK | | |
| | Use Case | UC | | |
| Metrics | Principle | PR | | |
| | Requirement | RQ | | |
| | Key Choice | KC | | |
| | Risk | RK | | |
| | Governance | GV | | |
| Functional Service | GUI Service | UI | | GUI mockup or screenshot |
| | App Logic Service | AS | | |
| | Data Service | DS | | |
| | Tech Service | TS | | |
| | Service Interface | SI | | |
| | Service Component | SC | | |

| Area/Category | Element Name | Abbr | Icon | Preferred Display |
|---|---|---|---|---|
| Infrastructure | Deployment Package | DP | | |
| | Middleware | MW | | Middleware product image |
| | System/Device | SY | | Emblematic image |
| | Node | ND | | Pictorial hardware embodiment |
| | Network | NW | | Emblematic network image |
| | Location | LO | | |
| Connection | Association | *AN* | | |
| | Flow | *FW* | | |
| | Composition | *CN* | | |
| | Realization | *RN* | | |
| General | Note | *NT* | | |
| | View Frame | VF | | |
| | Grouping | *GP* | | |
| | Generic Service | GS | | |
| | Generic Domain | DM | | |
| | — Transaction | | | |
| | — Clustering | | | |
| | — Environment | | | |
| | — Platform | | | |
| | — Region | | | |
| | — Tier | | | |
| | — Zone | | | |

| Area/Category | Element Name | Abbr | Icon | Preferred Display |
|---|---|---|---|---|
| Assistive Option | Cloud Service | CL | | |
| | Product | *PD* | | Shadow or product image |
| | Application | AP | | Unique application icon |
| | Mobile Device | MD | | Mobile device image |
| | DB Store | DB | | |
| | Composite – Process | PS | | |
| | Virtual Service | *VS* | | Dash or dotted boarder line |
| | Extension/Stereotype | EX | | Representative image |

Note:
— For simplicity, all elements are uniquely defined and shaped. The architecture elements are shown in black and white by default, and no formal semantics for colors. However, it's recommended to use color shades to distinguish the architectural elements in the same model view.
— The abbreviations in italic are not intended for visual presence.
— It's suggested to use preferred image, if possible, for better visual distinction among the same element type.
— An instance naming is denoted by a prefix-colon (e.g, :Apache). Multiple Instances are expressed using cardinality. For example, *Location (2)* is denoted as two similar locations.
— An element can contain sub-categories. For example, the *Requirement Element* also includes: RQ-NFR (non-functional requirement), RQ-RL (rule requirement), and so forth.
— The element property descriptions, as exemplified in this book, are practically short and clear, less restricted in syntactic structures.

# Appendix IV  Element Relationship

The following is a list of simplified connection relationships between elements for reference purpose.

| Element 1 | Element 2 | Relationship | Note |
|-----------|-----------|--------------|------|
| CP | Any | association | Any applicable elements |
| UC | TK | association | |
| UC | AS | association | |
| PR | CP | association | |
| SC | SI | association | |
| Any | SI | composition | Any exposed IT services |
| ND | DP | composition | |
| ND | MW | composition | |
| LO | ND | composition | |
| LO | SY | composition | |
| LO | NW | composition | |
| DP | Any | composition | Any IT services |
| ND | VN | composition | |
| VN | MW | composition | |
| DM | any | composition | |
| RO | UC | flow | |
| UI | AS | flow | |
| AS | DS | flow | |
| AS | TS | flow | |
| DS | TS | flow | |
| ND | NW | flow | |
| SY | NW | flow | |
| PR | KC | flow | |
| RQ | KC | flow | |
| RQ | UC | flow | |
| KC | RK | flow | |
| GV | KC | flow | |
| Any | SC | realization | Any IT services |
| SC | DP | realization | |

# Appendix V ArchiMate Mapping

In ArchiMate, the core framework or full framework is composed of a matrix of layers and aspects. In comparison, the A-ESA approach advocates a more agile and flexible architectural style and only contains five architecture areas: capability, architecture overview, case scenario, functional service, and infrastructure.

The A-ESA only adopts a minimal number of architectural elements. For those familiar with ArchiMate, the following is a quick comparison:

| # | ArchiMate Category | ArchiMate Element | A-ESA Representation |
|---|---|---|---|
| 1 | Stakeholder, Driver, and Assessment | Stakeholder | Directly related to the system architecture, and partly reflected by *Role*, and partly inferred from *Principle*, *Risk*, and *Note* |
| 2 | | Driver | Reflected from *Principle*, and *Requirement* |
| 3 | | Assessment | Reflected from *Capability, Risk, Note, Governance*, and *Key Choice* |
| 4 | Goal, Outcome, Principle, Requirement, and Constraint | Goal | Reflected from *Principle, Requirement,* and *Capability* |
| 5 | | Outcome | Reflected from *Capability, Risk, Note* |
| 6 | | Principle | *Principle* |
| 7 | | Requirement | Partly reflected by *Requirement* |
| 8 | | Constraint | Reflected from *Principle, Requirement, Governance,* and *Risk* |
| 9 | Meaning and Value | Meaning | Reflected from *Note* and *Extension* |
| 10 | | Value | Reflected from *Principle, Requirement, Key Choice, Note* and *Property Specification* |
| 11 | Strategy | Resource | Associated with *Capability* |
| 12 | | Capability | *Capability* |
| 13 | | Value Stream | Jointly reflected from *Composite Service/Process* and *Capability* |
| 14 | | Course of Action | Associated with *Capability*, and reflected from *Principle, Requirement,* |

| # | ArchiMate Category | ArchiMate Element | A-ESA Representation |
|---|---|---|---|
| | | | and *Key Choice* |
| 15 | Business Layer | Business Actor | Generalized as *Role* |
| 16 | | Business Role | Represented by *Role* |
| 17 | | Business Collaboration | Represented *Composite Service* or *Process* |
| 18 | | Business Interface | Materialized as *Service Component Interface* |
| 19 | | Business Process | Specified as *Composite Service* or *Process* |
| 20 | | Business Function | Represented by *Application Logic Service* |
| 21 | | Business Interaction | Represented by *Connection* |
| 22 | | Business Event | Specified from *Requirement* |
| 23 | | Business Service | Represented by *Task* or reflected from *Generic Service* |
| 24 | | Business Object | Aggregated as *Data Service* |
| 25 | | Contract | Defined by *Requirement* and is reflected from *Service Component Interface* |
| 26 | | Representation | Specified by *Generic Service, Data Service,* or *Extension – Document*, etc. |
| 27 | Composite | Product | *Product* |
| 28 | Application Layer | Application Component | Generalized by *Service Component* |
| 29 | | Application Collaboration | Represented by *Composite Service* or *Process,* or *Extension – Service Action* |
| 30 | | Application Interface | Specified as *Service Component Interface* |
| 31 | | Application Function | Specified as functional *Application Logic Service* |
| 32 | | Application Interaction | Represented by *Connection* or *Extension – Service Action* |
| 33 | | Application Process | Generalized as *Composite Service* or *Process* |
| 34 | | Application Event | Specified from *Requirement,* or represented by *Extension – Service Action* |
| 35 | | Application Service | Represented by *Application, Generic Service,* or *Application Logic Service* |
| 36 | | Data Object | Represented by coarse-grained *Data Service* |
| 37 | Technology Layer | Node | *Node* |

| # | ArchiMate Category | ArchiMate Element | A-ESA Representation |
|---|---|---|---|
| 38 | | Device | Represented by *System/Device* |
| 39 | | System Software | Specified as loosely-defined *Middleware* |
| 40 | | Technology Collaboration | Represented by *Extension – Service Action* |
| 41 | | Technology Interface | Specified as *Service Component Interface* |
| 42 | | Path | Represented by *Connection* |
| 43 | | Communication Network | Generalized as *Network* |
| 44 | | Technology Function | Specified as operational *Application Logic Service* |
| 45 | | Technology Process | Generalized as *Composite Service* or *Process* |
| 46 | | Technology Interaction | Represented by *Extension – Service Action* |
| 47 | | Technology Event | Specified from *Requirement*, or represented by *Extension – Service Action* |
| 48 | | Technology Service | Tech Service |
| 49 | | Artifact | Represented by *Extension – File & Medium* |
| 50 | Physical Elements | Equipment | Represented by *Extension – Non-IT Thing* |
| 51 | | Facility | Represented by *Extension – Non-IT Thing* |
| 52 | | Distribution Network | Network |
| 53 | | Material | Represented by *Extension – Non-IT Thing* |
| 54 | Implementation and Migration | Work Package | Targeted as *Deployment Package* |
| 55 | | Deliverable | Represented as *Service*, *Application*, *System*, *Product*, and *Capability* |
| 56 | | Implementation Event | Specified from *Requirement* and represented by *Note* |
| 57 | | Plateau | Captured from *View Frame* |
| 58 | | Gap | Represented by *Note*, or *Extension – File & Medium* |
| 59 | Other | Location | *Location* |
| 60 | | Logical Group | Logical *Group* |
| 61 | | Physical Group | Physical *Group* or Generic *Domain* |
| 62 | Connection | Composition | *Composition* |
| 63 | | Aggregation | Represented by *Composition* |

| # | ArchiMate Category | ArchiMate Element | A-ESA Representation |
|---|---|---|---|
| 64 | | Assignment | Represented by *Realization* |
| 65 | | Realization | *Realization* |
| 66 | | Serving | Represented by *Flow* |
| 67 | | Access | Represented by *Flow* |
| 68 | | Influence | Represented by *Flow* |
| 69 | | Association | *Association* |
| 70 | | Triggering | Represented by *Flow* |
| 71 | | Flow | *Flow* |
| 72 | | Specialization | Represented by *Realization* |
| 73 | | Junction | Represented by *Middleware* or *Connection* |
| — | | | Vide Appendix III for other unique A-ESA elements, including *Task, Use Case, Generic Service, Key Choice, Risk, Governance, GUI Service, Cloud Service, DB Store, View Frame, Extension, Application*, virtual elements (*Virtual Service, Virtual Node*), and *Domain*-associated elements (*Transaction, Clustering, Environment, Platform, Region, Tier*, etc.). |
| — | | | For simplicity, A-ESA does not emphasize the concepts of active structure, passive structure, behavior, motivation, and the like in the ArchiMate spec. |

In short, ArchiMate focuses on *enterprise architecture*, while A-ESA is about *enterprise solution architecture* featured with a more practical architectural-thinking framework for easier adoption.

# Appendix VI SOA Comparison

SOA is passé. It is an *architectural style* by intent, yet mistaken by many as web services, technical specs, or assets. A-ESA is a clearly defined IT service-based architecture, accommodating both SOA services and MSA [77] services, together with enterprise solution environment contemplations.

Here is a rough comparison between A-ESA and SOA with a corresponding set of elements.

| # | SOA Element | A-ESA Representation |
|---|---|---|
| 1 | Business Process | Composite Service/Process |
| 2 | Class Symbol | Extension – Class |
| 3 | Client Workstation | System/Device |
| 4 | Component | Service Component |
| 5 | Component-based Service Contract | Service Component Interface |
| 6 | Conflict | Risk/Issue |
| 7 | Database | DB Store |
| 8 | Design Principle | Architecture Principle |
| 9 | Generic Application | Application |
| 10 | Grid Service | Domain/Composite Service – Process/Middleware, depending on usage scenarios: |
| 11 | Human | Role |
| 12 | Human Readable Document | Extension – Document |
| 13 | Message | Data Service |
| 14 | Message Queue | Data Service |
| 15 | Physical Container | Node |
| 16 | Runtime Processing | Middleware/Package/Node |
| 17 | Service | Generic Service |
| 18 | Service Agent | Middleware/Tech Service |
| 19 | Service Composition | Composite Service/Process |
| 20 | Service Contract | Service Component Interface |
| 21 | Service Inventory | Package/Capability, Extension – Library |
| 22 | Service Inventory Container | Virtual Node |
| 23 | Service Layer | Domain, Group |

[77] Microservice Architecture

| # | SOA Element | A-ESA Representation |
|---|---|---|
| 24 | Service with State Data | Data Service – Caching |
| 25 | Strategic Goal | Architecture Principle |
| 26 | Transition Arrow | Flow Relationship |
| 27 | User Interface | GUI Service |
| 28 | Web Service | Functional Service |
| 29 | Web Service Boundary | Service Component Interface |
| 30 | Web Service Intermediary | Middleware, Tech Service |
| 31 | WS Policy Definition | Extension – Template |
| 32 | WSDL Definition | Extension – Template |
| 33 | XML Schema Definition | Extension – Template |
| 34 | Zone | Domain – Zone |

# Bibliography

1. **42010:2011: Systems and Software Engineering – Architecture Description**. ISO/IEC/IEEE, 2017.
2. **A Documentation Framework for Architecture Decisions**/U. van Heescha, P. Avgerioua, R. Hilliard. The Journal of Systems and Software, 2012.
3. **About the Unified Modeling Language Specification Version 2.5.1**. OMG, 2017.
4. **Application Architecture Guide 2.0: Designing Applications on the .NET Platform**/Meier, J.D., et al. Microsoft Corporation, 2008.
5. **Attributes Guided System Architecture Assessment**/Elias, George, et al. INCOSE, 2010.
6. **Building Evolutionary Architectures**/Ford, Neal, et al. O'Reilly, 2017.
7. **Can Middleware Survive the Serverless enabled Cloud?**/Perera, Srinath. hackernoon.com, 2018.
8. **Data Service Framework**/COSR. China CITIC Press, 2016.
9. **Defining "IT Service" for the IT4IT™ Reference Architecture**. The Open Group, 2019.
10. **Digital Doesn't Have to Be Disruptive: The Best Results Can Come From Adaptation Rather Than Reinvention**/Furr, Nathan, et al. Harvard Business Review, 2019.
11. **Domain-Driven Design: Tackling Complexity in the Heart of Software**/Evans, Eric. Addison Wesley, 2003.
12. **Enterprise Solution Architecture: An Overview**/Robertson, Bruce. Gartner Research, 2008.
13. **Everything You Need To Know About Microservices Design**/Kappagantula, Sahiti. edureka.co, 2019.
14. **General System Theory: Foundations, Development, Applications**/Ludwig Von Bertalanffy. George Braziller Inc., 2015.
15. **Implementing Cloud Design Patterns for AWS**/Keery, Sean, et al. Packt Publishing, 2019.
16. **Introduction to Solution Architecture**/McSweeney, Alan, ISBN-13:9781797567617, 2019.

17. **IT Governance: How to Reduce Costs and Improve Data Quality Through the Implementation of IT Governance**/Schindlwick, Helmut. CreateSpace, 2017.
18. **Mastering Archimate**/Wierda, Gerben. The Netherlands: R&A, 2014.
19. **Migrating Large-Scale Services to the Cloud**/Passmore, Eric. APRESS, 2016.
20. **Model-Based System Architecture**/Weilkiens, Tim., et al. Wiley, 2015.
21. **On the Criteria to be Used in Decomposing Systems into Modules**/Parnas, S. L. Carnegie Mellon University, 1972.
22. **Open Agile Architecture**. The Open Group, 2020.
23. **SDS Semantic Specification R3.0 – External Release**/Spaas, Philippe. IBM Corp, 2009.
24. **Service oriented architecture Modeling Language (SoaML) Specification**. OMG, 2012
25. **Service-oriented Enterprise Application Architecture**/Gu, C. BEIJING: Publishing House of Electronics Industry, 2013.
26. **Site Reliability Engineering: How Google Runs Production Systems**/Beyer, Betsy, et al. google.com, 2016.
27. **Solutions Architect's Handbook**/Shrivastava, Saurabh, et al. Packt, 2020.
28. **The Agile Architecture Revolution**/Boomberg, Jason. Wiley.
29. **The ArchiMate® 3.0.1 Specification: an Open Group Standard**. Open Group, 2018.
30. **The Architecture of Complexity**/Herbert A. Simon. Proceedings of the American Philosophical Society, 1962.
31. **The C4 model for Visualizing Software Architecture**/Brown, Simon. c4model.com, 2013.
32. **The Cathedral & the Bazaar**/Raymond, Eric. O'Reilly Media, 2001.
33. **The Elements of Style**/Strunk, William, et al. Allyn & Bacon, 2000
34. **The Model Thinker: What You Need to Know to Make Data Work for You**/Page, Scott E. Basic Books, 2019.
35. **The Open Group Agile Architecture Framework™**. The Open Group, 2019.
36. **The Timeless Way of Building**/Alexander, Christopher. Oxford University Press, 1979.

# ABOUT THE AUTHOR

Sean (Chunhong) Gu is a current certified Open Group Distinguished Architect with broad industry experience in international business, manufacturing, healthcare, and retail. Over the past 25 years, he has led a multitude of large-scale enterprise solution projects both in the USA and China, and has recently been focusing on IT strategic planning and enterprise solution architecture training. His previously published book, "Service-oriented Enterprise Application Architecture," drew from his numerous landing projects and sold well in China.

As part of the IT Architect Certification Board and a chief IT Architect instructor at IBM GCG, he has facilitated thousands of architects and technical leaders in China, the Asia-Pacific, the USA and Europe, and has mentored top-level executive architects for their career advancement.

Sean, graduated from the University of Chicago, holds Master's degrees in Physical Science, Systems Analysis, and Business Administration. He has a wide array of interests including swimming, hiking, calligraphy, and Chinese zither.

www.ingramcontent.com/pod-product-compliance
Lightning Source LLC
Chambersburg PA
CBHW051755200326
41597CB00025B/4558